"*The Perfect Investment* is extremely compelling. So much so, that as soon as I finished reading the book, I contacted Paul and said, "I'm in!" As an early stage entrepreneur that is always swinging for the fences on high-risk, high-growth startups, this is a much-needed wakeup call to balance my investment strategy with the highest return/lowest risk investment available. Well done, Paul!"

Wade Myers, Chairman of RealManage (an Inc 5000 tech-enabled real estate management firm), tech entrepreneur and investor, and Harvard MBA and case study author

❖

"I have known Paul Moore for almost 30 years. His business ethics are only surpassed by his innovative marketing ideas which are sure to help anyone seriously interested in this space."

Barry Farah. Real Estate Developer. CEO, Precocity - Dallas, TX

❖

"Paul has done a great job using his deep and valuable knowledge about Real Estate Investing to provide a very helpful resource for anyone looking at the opportunity to build wealth in multifamily. This is a book that can be utilized by those that may have never considered the opportunity before, but may stand to gain profitably with Paul's sound advice."

David Stevens, President & CEO Mortgage Bankers Association. Former US Assistant Secretary of Housing & Federal Housing Commissioner. Former Sr. VP Freddie Mac

✛

"Paul Moore has written a terrific book for real estate investors, new or experienced. He explains the benefits and provides a detailed but concise pathway based upon personal ex perience and in easy to understand language. A great recommendation for getting started in commercial real estate investment."

Allen Smith, Vice President Investments, Marcus & Millichap (top 10 US commercial brokerage – $33B Annual Sales)

✛

"The book is very impressive and complete. It goes beyond the basics and informs investors of all of the opportunities, and pitfalls, of investing in real estate. The ability for a potential investor, at any level of sophistication, to go to one location to access information about investing in multifamily real estate is very unique."

Rick Graf, President & CEO, Pinnacle Property Management Services (top 5 US property management firm – 146,000 apartment units under management)

✦

"As an investment advisor I am always seeking investments that will compliment the portfolio of a family or individual looking to grow their wealth without taking extraordinary risks. In this book, Paul builds a strong case for why multifamily housing provides a highly attractive risk to reward ratio on an investment you can actually touch and see!"

Micah Spruill, Managing Partner, Aurora Investment Advisors

✦

"Paul's career in real estate, his reputation as a trustworthy advisor, his niche in the recession-resistant multifamily sector, and his unique perspective on the true value of money make this book truly *The Perfect Investment*."

Ben Briggs, Executive Vice President, International Business. Briggs Freeman Sotheby's International Realty

❖

"*The Perfect Investment* is a great introduction for anyone looking to venture into commercial multi-family investing. Paul's approach during each step of the process is well defined and thoroughly explained. A perfect guide for the perfect investment."

Neal Golden, Vice Chairman and Texas Regional President of Newmark Grubb Knight Frank (top 3 US commercial brokerage – $100B annual sales)

❖

"When Paul sent me the first draft of this volume, his working title was *The Definitive Guide to Multifamily Investing*. Not bad - Except that I had yawned a bit. I couldn't shake the thought that it was more than that. 'Why not be more BOLD?' I asked. 'You should just call it what it really is... *The Perfect Investment!*'

Like this book's author, a man I am honored to count among my friends, I didn't start out thinking much at all about Multi-Family Properties or the Buy, Fix & Hold strategy in general (something silly about never wanting to be a 'Landlord'). I've spent my entire adult life in pursuit of the "Big Checks" wanting nothing more than to be a wildly successful Fix & Flip guy who would one day become the next great Real Estate Developer.

Then, I read this Book right as I was in the midst of, as the late great Dr. Wayne Dyer would say, making the 'Shift' from ambition to meaning in my own life. All at once I understood that I was climbing the wrong ladder to long-term, multi-generational "Success." I've discovered real Success is, much to the surprise of my younger self, *a way of life* more than the balance in a Swiss Bank Account.

My Business Partner and I want to do good and do well. We want the freedom to do what we want, when we want, without sacrificing our ability to be a present day provider. *The Perfect Investment* has carved a path for us to invest in something that will outlast us. This allows us to do things the right way by providing a predictably stable foundation on which our descendants can build their futures. That my friends, is what I call *The Perfect Investment,* and this book will show you how to turn this dream into your new reality!"

Joseph Mark Loud, Real Estate Developer
Aspiring Multi-Family Property Owner

✠

The Perfect Investment

Create Enduring Wealth from the Historic Shift to Multifamily Housing

Paul Moore

Additional copies of this book are available at:

www.perfectinvestmentbook.com

Or by contacting the author at
1-800-844-2188
P.O. Box 7301
Roanoke, VA 24019

Published by Paul Moore
Cover Design by Savanna Kahle
Edited by Carole McFarland

Table of Contents

ACKNOWLEDGEMENTS

I want to acknowledge and thank the Creator of the Universe for giving me life and breath and the opportunity to be an entrepreneur.

I want to thank Elaine, my beautiful wife of nearly 30 years, and my four amazing kids: Jonathon, Hannah, Mary Grace and Abby. Thanks for giving me the time and space to create!

I acknowledge the enduring debt I owe to Chad Doty, Dan Chamberlain and Kieran Donohue, the leaders of Multifamily Partner Program. They taught me the ropes and plowed the way for this guide.

FOREWORD
by Warren Taryle, CPA

Wow, what a great read! Now I know that is not the normal way to begin the foreword to a book (especially a real estate investing book), but this is not a normal book.

Early on in my tax career, I noticed something that all of the wealthiest clients I worked with had in common. It wasn't education, family line, or even a great attitude. It was that they all owned investment real estate of some type. What I did not know at the time was, "did the real estate make them wealthy or did they invest in real estate because they were wealthy?" The only thing I knew was that wealthy people held real estate investments and plenty of them. Over the many years of my CPA practice, I have learned the answer to that "chicken or the egg" question and I think once you finish reading this book, you will come up with the answer yourself.

As a tax strategist, the single best tool I have at my disposal to help my clients reduce their tax burden is rental real estate and the most efficient type of rental real estate is large multifamily properties. Sure, even single-family, three-bedroom, two-bath homes offer some tax benefit, but if you are looking to protect any type of real wealth, you must go multifamily and the bigger the better. If you have ever wondered how America's wealthiest families shelter much of their income from tax, you won't wonder any longer after you have read Paul's excellent chapter on tax. I know…an excellent chapter on tax? I did say this wasn't a normal book, didn't I?!

As I said, large multifamily real estate is the best tool I have in helping my clients to keep significant amounts of money that would have been otherwise paid in taxes. The challenge is the rather large knowledge gap most people have when it comes to this type of investment. Many can grasp the concept of single-family homes or duplexes, but when it comes to 100+ unit apartment complexes, I might as well tell them to build the first real estate development on Mars. That is why I was so excited that Paul decided to write this book.

In *The Perfect Investment*, Paul lays out, as only a trained engineer could, the facts about commercial real estate. Many real estate investment books are all too happy to have you put on your rose-colored glasses and read about how lucrative real estate investing is and how simple and risk-free it is as well. Paul, on the other hand, builds a strong case for commercial real estate by presenting all of the facts; both the good and the bad. Thereby actually allowing you to learn from his and many others' mistakes.

The Perfect Investment covers the obstacles to large multifamily real estate investing in a refreshingly honest way. He then presents a well thought out plan for making your way through the obstacle course in a way that only someone with Paul's years of experience could. As you would expect from a recovering engineer, Paul supplies you with the data and shows you how to analyze it. But the book does not stop there. It gives you sources to find the information for yourself and do your own analysis.

After Paul shows you the "WHY" he then goes into a detailed description of the "HOW." I, once, went into a large real estate investment where the bottom-line return was projected to be so large that I foolishly believed the *how* was not that important. Okay, stop laughing at me, it happens. As it turned out, the *how* really did matter and not only did I lose an unbelievable amount of money, the community was deprived of what would have been a very beneficial development. If only *The Perfect Investment* had been available for me to read then.

Warren Taryle, CPA MST
Founder Taryle Accounting CPA, PLLC
– Scottsdale, AZ

Introduction

I never planned to be a commercial real estate investor. As a matter of fact, I hated the thought of it.

I remember the first mall in my town growing up. It was a bustling hub of activity during my childhood. (It was said they had 29 shoe stores!) I used to walk its wide corridors as a child at Christmas. I couldn't wait to see Santa and give him my wish list.

Fast-forward 20 years…

I drove by that same mall during grad school. It looked more like a war zone. One anchor store was replaced with a flea market, and the DMV occupied another. Most of the stores were shut down, and the parking lot was filled with weeds, broken lights, and teenagers revving their muscle cars. Not a place I'd let my wife and daughters go near today.

The nice stores had moved to a new mall on the leading edge of town, and it appeared this formerly bustling mall was struggling to stay afloat.

I remember wondering about the fate of that poor guy who plowed millions into this sprawling complex.

I noticed the same thing at retail centers and office buildings. When I left Ford Motor Company to make my first run as an entrepreneur in Detroit, I excitedly clipped discounted office listings out of the newspaper. (For you Millennials, that was an antiquated form of communicating news using paper and ink.)

When I drove up, my heart sank. Another building that was sleek and modern in the 60s, now worn and mostly unoccupied in the 90s. "How do these building owners keep the lights on?" I wondered.

Certainly you've noticed the same phenomenon during the recent recession. How many half-finished subdivisions and condo projects graced the edge of your city? There were quite a few here. The most promising development in the region still sits mostly idle only two miles from my home.

So staking my fortune and future on commercial real estate is obviously not something I ever considered...

...Until I learned the truth about commercial multifamily investing.

When I left Ford Motor Company, I expected to run my HR outsourcing firm (a Professional Employer Organization – *aka PEO*) for the next several decades. I was a Finalist for Ernst and Young's *Michigan Entrepreneur of the Year* two years in a row, and I was making as much money as I thought my wife and I could reasonably spend.

Five years in to our startup turned successful venture, Wall Street got unexpectedly enamored with our business. PEOs were going public left and right, and achieving outrageous valuations along the way. A public company in Columbus, Ohio had tens of millions of cash on hand, and decided they wanted to expand into neighboring states.

We were their first acquisition, and I suddenly found myself with a few million dollars in cash and a cushy sales job working for the firm who acquired us.

Now it's nothing personal against my friends in Metro Detroit, but my wife and I had two young children and expected more (we added two more later), and we asked ourselves if this was the place we really wanted to raise them. My partner had already moved to Colorado Springs, and had a straight-on view of Pikes Peak. Another friend had moved to Charlotte and was loving it.

We ended up purchasing 120 acres in the heart of the Blue Ridge Mountains south of Roanoke Virginia. We built our dream home there on a mountaintop, complete with a huge stocked pond, walking trails through thick woods, an old tobacco barn, and old-fashioned cattle fencing.

We established a non-profit organization to reach out to international college students studying in the US and our children got the experience of having people from all over the world share our home and land. It was fun, but...

...I got bored pretty quickly.

Going into semi-retirement in your late 30's sounds exciting, but I was a high-energy entrepreneur and I couldn't sit still. I got involved in all types of investing, and I have to tell you that I essentially went back to school again for the next 17 years. I learned things I never learned in engineering school or my MBA. Though I had a lot of fun and made a lot of friends, *it's really not a school I'd ever want to repeat.*

That's one of the main reasons I wrote this guide.

I learned a lot about investing over the past few decades. I made a lot of money, but honestly, I lost a lot, too. More than I care to recount here. Some I can't recall (or choose not to).

Through this process, I've learned some lessons that can save you years of hard knocks... and a huge mound of cash. I've said this over and over to friends and investors, and I'll tell you straight...

If only I knew then what I know now about commercial multifamily investing, I would never have done anything else.

You don't have to re-learn what I've learned. This guide will help you pave a safe and profitable path to passively create multi-generational wealth through fractional multifamily investing.

Oh, and a note on the title...

With dozens of asset classes, and thousands of investment

types in the world, you may think it's a pretty bold claim to call one "***The Perfect Investment***." I agree.

Perhaps you think I'm arrogant at this point. I apologize in advance to those who maintain that conclusion after reading on.

If you'll give me a chance, however, I plan to prove my assertion to the majority of you. I'm not the only one who sees the world this way, and I believe you will join me in my conclusion within the first 50 pages.

Chapter 1 – The *Rest* of the Story

Remember Paul Harvey? I'd be driving on I-75 in rush hour Detroit traffic thinking about a million things or on my mobile phone. (Ok, it was actually called a bag phone then, and if you're not old enough to remember one, check out this picture of mine at our website: www.wellingscapital.com/firstphone.)

Anyway, I'd be in my own world, but when I heard Paul Harvey's commanding voice, my ears were riveted to the radio to hear "...*the rest of the story.*"

My story's not as interesting as some of Paul's, so if you want to get right to the meat of multifamily investing, you can skip this chapter and go straight to Chapter 3.

As I said earlier, I'd made a lot of money selling my company to a publicly traded firm. I was semi-retired and bored, and I had to find an outlet for my entrepreneurial zeal.

It's said that those who have money get opportunities to invest that the average individual can't imagine. Returns one can only dream of when reviewing his or her quarterly 401k statement.

That's absolutely true.

I could show you how my partner and I exceeded 100% annual ROI flipping single family homes. I could show how I got a 400% ROI using paid search marketing (pay-per-click – e.g. Google AdWords etc.) through an online real estate marketing portal I developed. I could show you closing statements demonstrating how another business partner and I made up to $100,000 per waterfront lot at a beautiful Blue Ridge resort called Smith Mountain Lake. (We bought overgrown lots, cleared them, got dock permits and resold them within months.) I could take you to a small subdivision I developed and made a quick 55% profit on, or another subdivision my friend and I developed and sold near North Dakota's Bakken oilfields for a 320% profit. I could show you a multifamily property we built from scratch in under a year that returned all of our capital plus a fabulous profit in the first two years. *It's also true that people with money have an outrageous number of opportunities to waste it through ground floor opportunities and other high-risk ventures. And scams.* Like I said earlier, I could easily get depressed by dwelling on the costly mistakes I've made along the way. Like the two times I've bought penny stock in companies with amazing patents that were months from blowing up. (They blew up alright, but not in the way I expected.) Or the Charlotte entrepreneur I invested with. He'd found an amazing way to make 2 to 3% profit *per month* with his international currency trading platform. (He's now serving 153 years in the federal pen, and won't tell the Feds or any of his 2,000+ investors where their $18 Million went.) Or the waterfront investment home I built and should have *made* a quick $80k on... but I *lost* $40k instead. (That scroungy little guy swore he was a drywall expert!)

There are more examples on each side of the equation. The great news for my family is that I made far more than I lost over these two decades of investing.

The great news for *you* is that you can stand on my shoulders. You can start at my ceiling.

You don't have to make the mistakes I made, and you can start a multi-generational cash flow and equity growth machine that will protect your principal, guard your time, minimize your taxes, and give you the life you dream of. I can show you how to get there.

I'm going to show you *The Perfect Investment*...

Chapter 2 – Tired of Swinging for the Fences?

"It's not how much money you make, but how much money you keep, how hard it works for you, and how many generations you keep it for."

Robert Kiyosaki – Author *Rich Dad Poor Dad*

If you're a millionaire by the time you're 40, but blow it all by age 50, you've gained nothing. Except the opportunity to start all over again.

Are you still swinging for the fences?

I hope not. But if you are, let me encourage you to stop. Right now. Whether you're 22 or 82. It is not a workable long-term strategy. It wasn't for me, and it won't be for you either.

Sure, there are rare people who defy the odds, and make it big. And many investors hit it out of the park once… but they get the taste for a repeat. Which often eludes them the rest of their life.

There comes a time in many investors' lives when swinging for the fence is no longer fun or profitable. When the elusive glitter is seen for the illusion that it really is.

Stories of those hitting grand slams abound, but that is why they're repeated. *Because they are the exceptions.*

For each of these stories, there are literally dozens who have swung away and caught nothing but air. And were left rebuilding for years to get back to where they were when they took that crazy plunge.

Which story do you think will be told in blogs and bars and real estate investing clubs?

(A) Johnny bought a home for 45 cents on the dollar, then while renovating found out it could be rezoned commercially. He went on to sell it for four times what he paid!

Or...

(B) Gary and his son began quietly buying apartment buildings. For years, they faithfully built this business. Never made a fortune in any one year, but over time, they became one of the wealthiest families in town.

By the way, Johnny's 300% profit story didn't include the slam dunk deal that went south... or the quick flip that turned into a slow nightmare landing him a job delivering pizzas for Domino's 'til he got back on his feet.

The Law of Risk and Return

This is elementary, but it's worth underscoring here.

Risk is proportional to potential return.

At least in the age in which we live, and the planet we inhabit. Look at the odds on the lottery ticket. Or the "beta" on stocks. Or the published success rate of making a million in multi-level marketing.

I don't think I can top these three paragraphs and graph from *Investopedia: "The risk/return tradeoff could easily be called the 'ability-to-sleep-at-night test.' While some people can handle the equivalent of financial skydiving without batting an eye, others are terrified to climb the financial ladder without a secure harness. Deciding what amount of risk you can take while remaining comfortable with your investments is very important.*

In the investing world, the dictionary definition of risk is the chance that an investment's actual return will be different than expected. Technically, this is measured in statistics by standard deviation. Risk means you have the possibility of losing some, or even all, of your original investment.

Low levels of uncertainty (low risk) are associated with low potential returns. High levels of uncertainty (high risk) are associated with high potential returns. The risk/return tradeoff is the balance between the desire for the lowest possible risk and the highest possible return. This is demonstrated graphically in the chart below. A higher standard deviation means a higher risk and higher possible return.

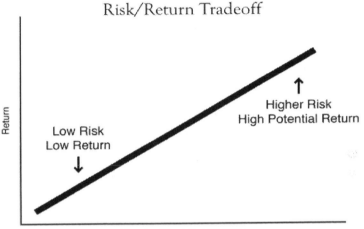

A common misconception is that higher risk equals greater return. The risk/return tradeoff tells us that the higher risk gives us the possibility of higher returns. There are no guarantees. Just as risk means higher potential returns, it also means higher potential losses."

(www.investopedia.com/university/concepts/concepts1.asp.
Accessed February 16, 2016)

Did you catch that? "The risk/return tradeoff tells us that the higher risk gives us the *possibility* of higher returns."

Don't roll the dice with your investment funds.

If you think investing is gambling, you will likely not retain your wealth long. Investment advisors typically advise their clients to allocate no more than about 10% of their funds to high-risk equities.

This should be money you can afford to lose. As one advisor told me, "Don't allocate any funds to high-risk ventures that you won't miss if alternatively used as kindling in your fireplace."

If you roll the dice with 50 or even 100% of your investible capital, and win, what about next time? And the following? This is simply not a sustainable strategy for 99% of the population. And not one that lends itself to commercial multifamily investing.

If that is your strategy, you should put down this book now and go bet on horses. You'll have no interest in where we're going.

In my first venture into commercial real estate, in the 90s, I invested with my partner who built a beautiful office building in a great location in Colorado Springs. Though it finished out nicer than expected... faster than planned... and under budget (even building through a Colorado winter and dealing with environmentalists over a rare breed of endangered mouse and 53 foot deep concrete piers...) we opened our doors not long before the 2000 downturn. Something we could not have anticipated or controlled. The profitability on that venture never approached what we planned. The project barely survived the first several years.

We made it through a very lean time, but here's the point: This high-risk/high *potential* return project was another example of the boom and bust mentality of a developer. If you want to invest that way, I hope it works out well for you. Many developers are among the world's wealthiest individuals. But I guarantee *many* more have ended in shambles, losing their wealth, their health and sadly, sometimes, their reputations and families.

It's important to get this straight... High risk does not lead to high return. It leads to high ***potential*** return. And equally true that it leads to high ***potential*** loss. You need to invest with an operator who will never gamble with your assets. One who won't play with your money. Never. Not a dime.

"Investing should be more like watching paint dry or watching grass grow. If you want excitement, take $800 and go to Las Vegas."

Paul Samuelson – *First American Winner of Nobel Prize in Economic Sciences*

Think about it… if you continue to play Double or Nothing, you may win a few times. But you will eventually land on nothing. And then what will you have left to play with next time around. You can do the math on that.

Bears prosper in some markets. Bulls prosper in other markets. But sooner or later, pigs will be consumed. I don't want to see this happen to you.

For the Long Haul.

Building multi-generational wealth through multifamily investing involves careful planning, diligence and patience. However, the gains you will receive over time are impressive. And the risk is surprisingly modest.

Successful multifamily investing has an eye on the distant horizon. But it has wonderfully stable cash flow from the first year or two, and the tax benefits are astounding.

Building a Multi-Generational Wealth Engine targets wealth for decades, or longer, and gives no thought to one-time gains. Successful multifamily investors are aiming at generations they may never see. An opportunity to leave a legacy.

"Wealth gained hastily will dwindle, but whoever gathers

little by little will increase it."

Solomon – *Proverbs 13:11*

Chapter 3 – Enduring Wealth is No Accident

It's really no secret. The super-wealthy perpetuate their fortunes by investing in assets the average investor has no practical access to. And by accessing tax breaks designed for them by their friends on Capitol Hill.

It's also no secret that many of the Forbes wealthiest list made their fortunes through commercial real estate. And a recent survey of high net worth investors found that 83% believe that commercial real estate assets will post better performance than equities for the rest of this decade. And later in this volume, I will show you statistics demonstrating that the risk/return ratio on commercial multifamily investing is about 400% better than the stock market.

So what holds most of us back?

Even a cursory review of the commercial real estate realm informs us that the vast majority of us cannot get meaningful access to this profitable investment class. Especially in a way that doesn't come with the burden of crushing debt and massive time commitment.

And if you don't know what you're doing, you could get burned.

Why You're Not Invited to Their Party

When I was in business school, we learned about the importance of erecting strategic barriers to entry around our products or companies. How could we assure that competitors were blocked from entering our space?

Some rely on patents. Some on controlling a scarce resource. High setup costs or R&D costs can keep competitors out. So can predatory pricing, brand loyalty and vertical integration.

Barriers to entry are obviously great for those who erect them. And frustrating to those on the outside.

The barriers to entry in commercial multifamily investing are significant. You cannot easily enter this space.

Sorry if the book title got your hopes up. This is not a path to easy wealth.

Then again it could be. *If you find someone who's already inside the barrier.* More on that later.

So what are some of these barriers to entry? Why is it so hard to enter this space?

Barrier #1: Cash Requirements

How big is your piggy bank? The cash required for projects of profitable scale is very high.

Have you seen those "make a fortune in real estate with no money down infomercials?" I guess that's possible, but I've been deeply entrenched in many aspects of real estate for a long time, and I've only seen a few deals like that.

Though they may exist somewhere, low or no money down deals essentially don't exist in the realm of safe, profitable, repeatable multifamily investing.

We'll talk about safe, profitable scale in a moment. But suffice it to say that the scale is in the 100+ apartment unit range, and properties like that typically cost at least $5 Million and usually much more. Let's say $10 Million plus in general. You will need to put about 25% down, or at least $2.5 Million. You will also need cash to make lender-mandated repairs, implement improvements to increase rents and maintain mortgage payment and repair reserves.

So you should consider $3.5 Million or more as a good

starting point *for one project*. With a certain degree of diversification you can help the overall stability of your portfolio. So hopefully you've got something like $7 to $10 million or more in total assets to get in. Many of you have this available. But unless you're paying cash, that still won't get you through the door. You need to qualify for debt financing...

Barrier #2: Loan Qualifications

Multifamily Experience Required. Remember that whiney college kid in the old TV commercial? The big shot behind the desk informed him that: "Experience is required for this job." He turned to the camera with a bewildered shrug and said, "But how do I get that experience?"

This is a quandary for aspiring multifamily investors. You may reason that you need to start small and build up to large. But one of my many goals in this book is to convince you <u>not</u> to go out and start buying small apartments. Starting with a four-plex, a twelve-unit, or even a few dozen units could be a sure path to drive you out of this business quickly. (And I won't give you your money back for this book!)

Seriously, you need to have credible experience for at least three reasons:

(1) The lender looks carefully at your experience. (It's not like buying your first home. Imagine the lender asking, "So how many times have you successfully rented anyway, young lady?") Banks have this thing for wanting to get their money back, and experience is a big indicator.

(2) The broker and seller will scrutinize you. Again, unlike residential realtors, commercial realtors do not have to present every offer to the sellers. They will only give

the time of day to those who they believe will put food on their table. And they will not bother with someone who they think can't close... and could ruin the sale for their seller and them. (Much more on this later.)

(3) You will need this experience to successfully operate the property. (Did I hear you call me *Captain Obvious?*)

In addition to requiring significant multifamily experience, lenders will want to see a massive personal balance sheet. Even non-recourse lenders will typically require personal assets equal to at least half the balance of the loan.

Did you catch that? In addition to the value of the asset you're purchasing, lenders may want to see other assets totaling at least half the value of the loan you are applying for. This can be from you or others you can get to sign for the loan.

In the $10 Million/75% Loan-to-Value example from above, this means the buyer must come up with about $3.5 Million or so in cash to put down and make repairs, etc... and have significant other liquid assets for debt service required by the lender.

This is not to mention a clear track record, great credit score, no bankruptcies or short sales, etc. This is not a set formula and it varies by situation and lender, but trust me when I say that this is a significant barrier for most investors.

Barrier #3: Commercial Brokers

It's all about who you know. As I said, in contrast to residential realtors, commercial brokers are not required to present all offers to their sellers. *And they don't.* Brokers typically work with a small pool of experienced buyers who they know will be able to close deals.

Crowdfunding – Millions of Investors' Hopes Dashed

I mentioned our friends on Capitol Hill a few pages back. Several years ago, Congress tacked on an amendment to the Jobs Act that should have opened the door for tens of millions of average investors to gain access to large-scale investments, the type typically only accessed by the wealthy. Bravo!

Apparently the Securities & Exchange Commission was not too happy about putting this much choice and control in the hands of "the ignorant masses." Charged with enacting rules to oversee the new regulations, over three long years later, they finally released the new regulations.

In summary, they made this process so burdensome, so cumbersome, so paperwork-heavy, that according to many, they effectively undermined the very laws they were charged with enforcing. According to preliminary interpretations, the new regs make it virtually impractical for the average small to mid-sized business or investment fund to grant access to the average American who wants to invest.

My business partner and I built a beautiful Hyatt House hotel in the Midwest some years ago. After studying the powerful market fundamentals in Texas, we decided Houston would be our next target city.

I spent some time on the ground there, and after studying a variety of land parcels, we wrote up a Letter of Intent to buy a certain commercial parcel near the heart of the booming Texas Medical Center.

We offered nearly full price (about $7 million per acre) and submitted it to the owner through his broker. Days went by. Then more than a week. We were surprised they hadn't accepted or countered our offer right away. When I finally got the broker on the phone, it became fairly obvious that he hadn't even presented it to the seller. Or at least the seller paid it little mind.

I was flabbergasted. Offended. *Didn't he know who we were?*

That's exactly the point.

He had no idea who we were. And he was too busy to find out. In his mind, we didn't seem like people who would put food on his table or gas in his BMW, so we were initially ignored. (He found out about our experience later, and eagerly sought us out to buy that parcel.)

It's not just who you know... it's also about what you've done. As with lenders, commercial brokers want to see experience, other assets owned and operated, and a positive track record from offer to close and beyond. They will ask for references and pointedly inquire about how many other accepted offers you closed or failed to close on and why. They will ask you where your equity is coming from, how you know you can qualify for debt, and even details on your financial projections for the property.

One client, or even one large deal, may provide the majority of the broker's annual income, and they refuse to take any risks dealing with unknown buyers. The risks of not closing mean that they will have egg on their face and have to go back to the buyer pool to seek a new offer. This will raise concerns about the property and could easily result in delays, missed loan payoff deadlines, and a lower price.

Even if the buyer is positioned to close, the broker will want to assure that this buyer won't significantly "re-trade" on the way to closing. This can result when an uninformed buyer gets bad news during inspections and tries to renegotiate with the seller. (Or they are just trying to save money by renegotiating.) This can be very frustrating and costly for the broker and seller, and they want to avoid buyers with this reputation.

Brokers will frequently advise their sellers to take a lower offer from a *known buyer*. They often do. Heightening this barrier for the rest of the world who are not in their inner circle. Like other barriers, it's possible to overcome this. But it's by no means automatic (we'll discuss these key issues much more toward the end of this guide).

The Multifamily Sales Process

In the residential real estate world, the arena that most homebuyers are familiar with, there is typically a listing agent and a buyer's agent. Usually these are two different individuals. There are strict rules that each party must play by. Offers must be treated with strict confidentiality right up through closing.

Not so in the commercial world. Typically the commercial seller's broker is the only broker in the transaction, and he sifts through buyers and offers at his discretion. Commercial brokers serve as gatekeepers to determine which buyers are legit and which are not. Brokers don't have to present the high offer, or any offer for that matter. Brokers can talk to prospective buyers about what they're hearing from other buyers, and they can relay where the other offers are with the goal of getting the best price for their sellers.

Most commercial multifamily properties are offered in an auction style basis. This means that there is no set price established by the seller. They allow the market to establish a price and they decide if they will accept the best offer. The seller's broker typically communicates the seller's price expectation through a "whisper price." Prospective buyers analyze and bid accordingly.

Barrier #4: Economies of Scale

Go Big or Go Home. Economies of Scale start at a very high level. When I started to see the remarkable demographic trends that are driving the multifamily sector, I immediately considered purchasing a six-unit apartment building in a nice part of town. It wasn't on the market, it was fully leased, and no big problems surfaced in my cursory reviews. I talked to the owner personally...

"This seems profitable to you, ma'am. Why are you selling?"

"Well, I'm just tired. Tired of screening tenants, tired of Saturday calls, tired of trying to be both a mom *and* property manager. I'm trying to start a new medical business and I can't do everything. But you could probably pull it off since you've been in real estate a long time."

A pretty standard answer among sellers of small properties. Yes, many get an off-site property manager. And that can work. But the cost per unit to run a small complex is much more than a large one. A large complex can afford an on-site staff, and that's one way economies of scale really kick in.

Many operators see this economy starting at about 100 units. Some would say 200. Some much higher. The economies of scale at 200 are certainly better than 100. For example, the property manager's salary on a 200-unit complex isn't much higher than that of the 100-unit manager. The marketing on a 200-unit property may be similar to that on a 100-unit property as well. There are many other ways the scale works in favor of the large property owner. Which is effectively another barrier to a new investor in this space.

Large properties also have access to multiple streams of income that are unavailable to the small owner. For example, large properties (particularly portfolios) can set up a cooperative insurance policy for renters' insurance. New renters add $10 or so per month to their rent to buy their insurance. But up to $5 of that comes back to the property owner if claims are low. This can really add up and increase property value, as we will see later. Large properties can also negotiate cable and Internet deals that allow them to share in those revenues. This can be quite substantial as well.

You may find this hard to believe, but I'll prove it later. Please take my math on faith for now. A 200-unit property where 65% of the renters buy in-house renters' insurance (only $5/mo. net revenue) and 75% of the tenants sign up for Internet and cable (say $25/mo. revenue) will increase their revenue by $52,800 annually. At a 6.5% cap rate, **these simple items translate to an increase in asset value of over $800,000.**

This is equity in the owner's pocket at the time of refinance or sale. Hopefully this gives you a preview of the power of professionally owned commercial multifamily. And I hope it encourages you to skip over the small properties and figure out how to go big.

Unlike many businesses, this is not one you can easily tiptoe into part time. This is why most don't. **And that's just the way the insiders want to keep it.**

So how *do* you get access?

I didn't write this book about *The Perfect Investment* just to frustrate you. There are meaningful ways to access the historic returns, principal safety, and powerful tax management strategies enjoyed by commercial multifamily property owners. I promise we'll get there. But first, let's talk about the demographic trends driving the historic growth of this asset class.

Chapter 4 – It's All in the Numbers

Demographic Trends Driving the Explosive Growth in Multifamily Investing

Vanderbilt. Rockefeller. Carnegie. Gates. Buffet.

Household names. These legendary moguls were able to read demographic trends and apply the technology of their day to provide solutions that resulted in extreme wealth. Wealth that would transcend generations. Products and wealth that would benefit millions around the world.

> By the way, if your goal is to accumulate and perpetuate massive multi-generational wealth, there will obviously be many ups & downs along that path. Start today by asking yourself "WHY?" Why do you want to do this? Then set that goal before you and run after it with all your heart. If you're curious about my BIG WHY, check it out in Appendix C.

About the time I turned 50, I looked over my life. Where had I succeeded? Where had I failed? What aspects of these business ventures did I want to replicate? Which ones did I want to run from?

And what business and/or investment class would be a fit for my goals? I realized that the boom or bust cycle that most entrepreneurs operated on was not something that I wanted to continue through the last half of my life. I wanted to invest in an asset class that was safe, stable, predictable, evergreen, and based on strong and long trends that had nothing to do with a war in the Middle East, the latest technology breakthrough, or the mood on Wall Street this month.

I wanted something with demographic trends that would last the rest of my lifetime, and likely through my children's. A perfect investment.

Now that's a tall order.

In the last decade, when new horizontal drilling technologies opened up a wild increase in the ability to extract oil from hard-to-access rock, places like the Bakken oil fields of North Dakota exploded. Posted job openings exceeded 18,000, and thousands slept in their trucks or set up tents in this harsh environment.

I saw it first hand. Hotels, motels, mancamps, RV parks, condos, townhomes and apartments popped up all over the plains. It was literally amazing to watch former prairie towns like Watford City go from 2,000 to about 10,000 almost overnight.

Some North Dakotans recalled the 50s boom and bust cycle, and they warned about what could happen. More remembered a similar cycle in the early 80s.

But North Dakota had rocketed past California and Alaska to become the second-highest oil producing state, and the press and many well-meaning bloggers proclaimed:

This is *Not* a Boom… This is an Industry!

So everyone "knew" that oil prices wouldn't retreat below the recent range of $80 to $100 per barrel, right? And most of the developers who poured millions into real estate there ignored the simple laws of supply and demand (both for oil production and real estate availability), as well as the lack of diversity of the economy, as well as… well, you get the picture.

There were 18,000 job openings, so if we build it, they will come.

Yeah right. You probably know the rest of the story. If not check it out here: www.wellingscapital.com/boom-bust

Anyway, I was 50, and certain I wanted to stop swinging for the fences. I was eager to find something stable and profitable. I wanted something I could count on for decades and beyond. Something I could teach my children. Something that would give them some of the same opportunities I've been blessed with, but without the painful learning curve that I (and most entrepreneurs I know) endured.

I found that opportunity in commercial multifamily investing. And the strength and length of demographic trends are one of the most important factors that caused me to invest my time, talent and resources into this space.

I'm not alone. The national press has been buzzing about multifamily investing for the past several years. A steady stream of headlines tell the tale...

➤ **The U.S. Rental Market is On Fire**

➤ **Multifamily Sector Sees New Confidence and Securitization**

➤ **The Apartment Boom: Multifamily Continues at a Torrid Pace**

➤ **US Multifamily Investment Enjoys Record-Breaking Year, Tops $139 Billion**

So what are the demographic trends that are causing the significant growth in multifamily investing? As you review these, please note *both the strength and the length* of these trends. They're not going away any time soon, and in fact they appear to be increasing.

The Big Picture

Rental housing in general is synced to one obvious key driver: the number of renter households. As the number of renters in the nation, or a market, or a submarket increase, the multifamily business becomes more profitable and attractive.

You may say, "Yeah, like North Dakota, right? What happens when millions of new units are built? And renting goes out of style again?"

Great point, reader! Those are the types of questions I was asking when I entered this space. Hang with me.

According to John Burns Consulting, new renter households were forming at 7.7 times the rate of new construction from 2010 through at least 2015. Think about it. During the same years that people were losing their homes to foreclosure (and therefore moving into rentals)... their average wages were dropping,,, and credit markets were tightening for *all new construction*. Which included multifamily.

This caused a significant new apartment supply and demand imbalance. Since most everyone who can afford it prefers newer and nice, this imbalance obviously trickled straight down from new properties to existing, and owners have been scrambling to update their units and raise their rents. Which has trickled down further into older, uglier properties, single family homes, condos and more. The multifamily industry has expanded rapidly.

This imbalance is partially due to the increase in US population for sure. But that's not all, because...

Home ownership is significantly declining in the US.

When I was first introduced to this stat, I was suspicious. Is this a temporary setback in homeownership? Strictly a result of the recession? That played a role, but if you look at the long-term trend, it is simply returning to more of a norm after a decade-long failed experiment in government tampering from 1995 to 2005.

You see, in the mid-90s, the federal government, in its great wisdom, thought it best that many more of its citizens stop renting and fulfill the American Dream of homeownership. So they passed legislation that significantly lowered the bar for people with marginal credit, no savings, and lower wages to buy a home. Sometimes a very nice home.

You remember ARMs, stated income and no-doc programs, right? "Just write down whatever you want on the loan app, and we won't even check it. Congratulations on your new home!"

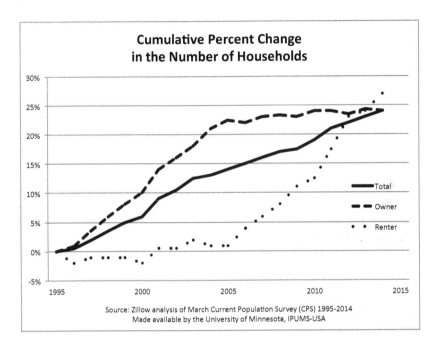

Cumulative Percent Change in the Number of Households

Source: Zillow analysis of March Current Population Survey (CPS) 1995-2014
Made available by the University of Minnesota, IPUMS-USA

I know someone who earned about $50k per year who bought a 7,000 square foot old mansion for $600,000. *As a second home!* His plan was to get cash back from seller at closing, invest that cash in a trading system he studied, then use the profits from trading to fund his mortgage payments. He didn't have the home for long till the bank got it back.

Needless to say, once folks started... then stopped... making payments, it caused a bad situation. Then the economy slowed, incomes dropped and home values plummeted. Millions who had qualified for... then purchased homes... lost their homes and returned to the renter pool. (This includes the guy with the second mansion. He not only lost the mansion, but was forced to ditch his family's primary home, and they moved to a two-bedroom apartment.) Home ownership normalized again, and of course the government blamed *those mean bankers.*

The homeownership rate, which peaked above 69% in 2005, has returned to a more normal rate around 63%. And it continues to drop. Check out this graph...

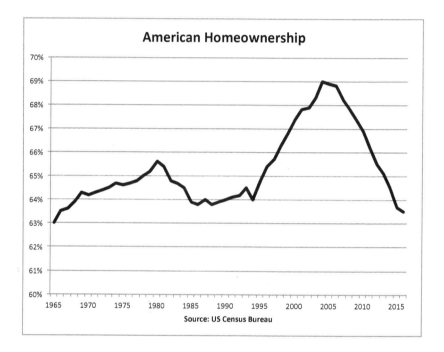

American Homeownership

Source: US Census Bureau

Note that every 1% decline in the homeownership rate translates to about a million new renters. Will we eventually be like Germany, with home ownership rates in the 40-50% range?

Also consider that this historical snapshot demonstrates another fact I really like about multifamily investing: it has a built-in buffering feature in down economies. While there was certainly downward pressure on rents in the 2009-12 era, that pressure was offset by the fact that millions of former home-owners had suddenly become renters. The multifamily business did not suffer to the degree of the housing market in general. And it recovered far more quickly.

The national default rate on multifamily loans is very low. If you take out the four sand states (CA, NV, AZ, FL) with the largest boom-bust cycles, the default rate drops even more. The rate is even lower in stable markets with balanced supply and demand. Top operators with good property managers do much better than this.

Check out the following graphic showing serious delinquency rates from the Housing Finance Policy Center's 2015 chart book. As you can see, the Freddie Mac delinquencies (60 days late on mortgage payments) peaked for single family homes at about 4% in late 2009. (FHA loan delinquencies actually hit about 9%.) About the same time, Freddie Mac's multifamily delinquency rates peaked at only about 0.4%.

At the time of this report, Freddie Mac residential delinquency rates were just below 2%. At the same time, multifamily delinquencies sat at a mere 0.03 to 0.05%.

So the multifamily delinquency rate... at its peak... was 90% lower than the residential rate in the worst downturn since the Great Depression. Then it retreated further to about 98% lower than the residential delinquency rate by early 2015. Did you catch that? Another reason to love the multifamily sector!

Check it out:

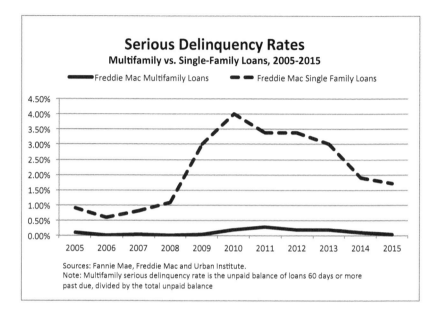

If you would like to see this whole 36-page report, go to our website: www.wellingscapital.com/delinquency-rates.

I was impressed with all of these statistics, but I was curious. Why? What has driven this spike, and why should I believe it would continue? To answer that, we need to look at the fundamentals driving this trend. I will review several here.

Multifamily Demographic Driver #1: Baby Boomers are flocking to rental housing.

The Baby Boomers are the nation's second largest demographic group ever. This group consists of individuals born between 1946 and about 1964.

As of the 2010 US Census, about 77 million baby boomers were alive and kicking. Dramatically increasing lifespans mean that this group will play a major role in the economy for many years to come.

"But don't Boomers typically own their homes?"

Not as much as you may think. For a variety of reasons, Boomers have been selling (or losing) their homes and renting. Polls and stats say that on average, when they return to renting, *they never buy again.*

Wealthier baby boomers shun homeownership

Excerpts from CNBC article: "The U.S. home ownership rate is at the lowest level in 25 years and is widely expected to go even lower. That's not just the result of younger Americans struggling to make ends meet to save for a down payment... It is increasingly the result of middle-aged, higher income Americans choosing to rent.

Renter growth is now at the highest level in 30 years, and families or married couples ages 45–64 accounted for about twice the share of renter growth as households under age 35, according to a new study by the Joint Center for Housing Studies at Harvard University. In addition, households in the top half of the income distribution, although generally more likely to own, contributed 43 percent of the growth in renters.

Duncan pointed to demographics. Baby boomers are now moving out of their homeownership years, while Generation X, a smaller group by 6 million to 7 million, also has a growing preference to rent after being hit hard during the recession, losing income, credit and even their homes.

Because of that, rental apartment occupancy is now at an all-time high, and rents are rising at twice the pace of inflation. In turn, that is putting pressure on renters young and old, but not necessarily pushing them to homeownership. Higher rents mean it is more difficult to save for a down payment."

www.cnbc.com/2015/06/24/wealthier-baby-boomers-shun-homeownership.html (Accessed July 11, 2016)

Multifamily Demographic Driver #2: The nation's largest demographic group is choosing or being forced into rental housing.

Echo Boomers now top the Baby Boomers at about 80 million

strong. This is the census block group born in the 80s and 90s, also called Generation Y or Millennials.

Note that the high foreclosure rate on single family homes was in spite of government intervention trying to save homeowners from foreclosure. A benefit not necessarily afforded to commercial property owners. Here is a quote from Freddie Mac's Multifamily Research Perspectives 2012, in the midst of the recession...

"The percentage of loans in foreclosure proceedings can be used as a measure of single-family housing market conditions. Based on MBA's (Mortgage Bankers Association) National Delinquency Survey, the foreclosure rate has skyrocketed from around 1% in late 2005 to a historical high of 4.6% by 2010; since then it has decreased from the peak but is still at an elevated level of 4.3%. Foreclosures increase both the supply of housing available and the demand for housing. Even with economic growth we do not expect a rapid decline of the foreclosure rate. Over the past several years, the pipeline of non-performing mortgages to be resolved has become large. In addition to various government efforts to reduce distressed sales, delayed bank repossessions, legal issues, property maintenance, and other issues continue to complicate and slow down the current foreclosure process. There are still 1.4 million foreclosures in process and an even higher number of underwater mortgages (11 million) according to the CoreLogic 2012 May Foreclosure Report. Generally, a higher foreclosure rate is an indicator of a weaker homeownership market. We expect high foreclosure volumes to continue."

This group makes up the bulk of recent new household formation, and their propensity to buy homes is surprisingly low. While new US households have typically bought vs. rented at a 65/35 ratio, the past several years have seen a striking reversal: new households are now owning vs. renting at a 25/75 ratio.

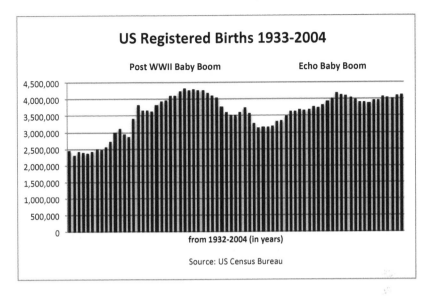

US Registered Births 1933-2004

Post WWII Baby Boom   Echo Baby Boom

from 1932-2004 (in years)

Source: US Census Bureau

Echo Boomers are largely disenfranchised with the concept of homeownership. They watched their friends and parents lose their homes in the recent recession. After many grew up believing a home was the cornerstone of their investment portfolio, they watched this "fact" dissolve into a myth before their very eyes.

> "Since 2005, an average of 804,000 new renter households per year have been created compared to just 75,000 per year from 1990 to 2004. That's a stunning annual increase of 1,040%, inverting the ratio of homeowner/rental household formation to 25/75 from its historic ratio of 65/35."
> - HUD & US Census

Gen Y'ers want a more flexible lifestyle. They are less likely to stay in one job, one home, or one city. Why lock oneself into a 30-year contract to a seemingly overpriced home and forego the flexibility to pick and move for a better job or new friends next year? Access to public transportation is better from many multifamily properties, and even a car means insurance, repairs, gridlocked traffic, and environmental consequences.

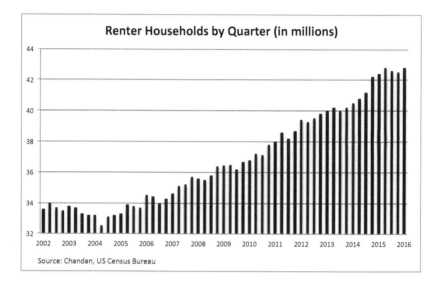

Renter Households by Quarter (in millions)

Source: Chandan, US Census Bureau

A study by GoBankingRates found that "62% of Americans have less than $1,000 in their savings accounts and a third of those under-savers have no savings account at all. The most frequently selected amount that people say they have in savings is zero. 28% selected this answer. Even worse, the next-most-common answer is 'I don't have a savings account,' selected by one in five people (20.7%)."
www.gobankingrates.com/savings-account/62-percent-americans-under-1000-savings-survey-finds/ (Accessed February 16, 2016)

Millennials also carry a record debt load. Student debt is at an alarming level, and this generation doesn't appear to place a big value on saving up money. This would have mattered little in purchasing a home a decade ago, but the crash has tightened lending restrictions back toward the historical norm. But this generation's savings and other debt are anything but the norm.

Why Millennials Love Renting

Excerpts from Forbes Article:

"With Millennials facing an unemployment rate of more than 8% and $1 trillion in student loan debt, they're increasingly renting instead of buying homes. In fact, the true home ownership rate for 18-34 year-olds has fallen to a new low: 13.2%. But finances aren't the only reason for the dip in homeownership. Millennials are recognizing the many benefits of renting — including reasons that have nothing to do with money."

The article goes on to detail benefits in the following categories...

1. Love of Amenities
2. Love of Community
3. Love of Flexibility
4. Love of Convenience

"The ultimate benefit of renting may arise from the flexibility of leaving for any reason, especially career reasons. Millennials tend to change jobs three times more often than their older counterparts and stay with the same employer for just three years on average, according to the U.S. Bureau of Labor Statistics. Renting instead of buying makes transferring to a new or better job much simpler. Some leases may even include a termination clause that specifies acceptable reasons for early termination, such as a job transfer that is more than 50 miles away. In some cases, the tenant may not be liable for any payment if the unit is re-rented within a particular time period."

www.forbes.com/sites/trulia/2014/10/07/why-millennials-love-renting/#46f9f5d-f1447 (Accessed July 11, 2016)

Multifamily Demographic Driver #3: US immigration continues to grow.

As a group, US immigrants, regardless of source location or socioeconomics, rent more often than they own, and rent for longer periods of time.

A Harvard housing study said, "About half of all immigrants are renters, including 74 percent of those under age 35." *www.jchs.harvard.edu/sites/jchs.harvard.edu/files/ahr2011-3-demographics.pdf (Accessed July 14, 2016)*

Check out this graph showing the effect that immigration is having on the US population. Assuming that immigrants continue to prefer renting at a higher percentage than non-immigrants, it will be hard to over-estimate the impact of this powerful driver.

Demographic Shift due to Mass Immigration
(in millions)

Legend:
- Growth Caused by Post-1970 Immigration
- Growth from Population Already in US, 1970

Source: 37th Parallel Properties (www.37parallel.com)

Conclusion: This is big. Really big. Finally sold on multifamily – The Perfect Investment!

So I was thoroughly convinced by the demographics that the multifamily business had a sound future. The numbers show a strength and undeniable length that should go on long after my lifetime.

Now that I believed in the business, what type of multifamily property should I invest in? I am an entrepreneur, and I wanted a business plan to map out my direction. I'll tell you about the powerful wealth-expanding multifamily strategy that my partners and I are pursuing in the next chapter.

From the Study: "The Access of Immigrants to the Homeownership Market"

"Immigrants can also have a lower access to the housing and credit markets. They lack information on these markets and they may suffer from discrimination affecting not only the screening of housing units but also the type of mortgage and insurance made available to them. Even if some immigrants access homeownership, they may be more vulnerable to adverse economic shocks that could make them default on their mortgage and force them to resell their dwelling.

...staying in the rental sector can be a choice for some immigrants who prefer to make financial transfers to their family in their home country or accumulate wealth to purchase a dwelling in their home country after return migration."

www.voxeu.org/article/immigrants-and-homeownership.
(Accessed July 11, 2016)

One final note: Demographics change over time. I've made the case that trends driving multifamily are deep and lasting, but you may wonder if this is still true upon reading this book. Check out the latest demographic trends at www.wellingscapital.com/demographics.

Chapter 5 – Toilets, Tenants & Trash

I always cringed when I heard the tales of rental property owners. I pictured the 3am phone calls for overflowing toilets. The eviction notices tacked to the door and the ensuing confrontations with tenants. I even recalled my one experience with sub-leasing my apartment as a newlywed...

We had just moved to Detroit to work at Ford Motor Company. My wife and I were happy to lease a two-bedroom apartment at Village Green Apartments, in Southgate, Michigan. Seven months into our lease, we decided it made sense to buy, and we found a perfect little bungalow a few miles away.

We were committed to fulfilling our lease, so we placed an ad to sublease our apartment. The kid seemed nice enough, and the property manager approved his credit. We handed over the keys with little thought to the many ways this could go south. (After all, I'd just finished six years of college, and I knew all I needed to know about life and real estate, right?)

The guy made the first two payments on time and all seemed well. Then he was really late on the third, and even later on the fourth. I had to go to the door one time, and a quick glance over his shoulder told me there was more to this guy than met the eye. There was trash strewn all over the living room. I mean *all over.* And it was deep. I couldn't tell what it was, but something was definitely amiss.

We continued to get late payments, and if I recall correctly, he didn't make the final one or two payments in full. When he finally moved out, the property manager called to say he had left the place in an absolute shambles. *How could one guy make this much mess in only five months?* (Too bad the *Hoarders* show hadn't been conceived yet.) I lost my $500 deposit and I considered myself fortunate that I wasn't charged for damages.

Another time I bought a nice doublewide to fix and flip –

about two hours from my home in Southwest Virginia. The economy slowed down, and I couldn't sell it. I finally agreed to a rent-to-own for a sincere young couple. (I hate renting single family homes on a small scale, because a single vacancy translates to 100% vacancy in that asset.) They would take care of all repairs and maintenance and I would have little or no reason to ever make the long trek there to visit them (any more than a Wells Fargo exec would come to check on your mortgaged home).

As in almost every rent-to-own situation, this family struggled for years to get their credit up and qualify for a mortgage (to buy me out as planned). I really didn't mind, though, because I had spent $40,000 on a $65,000 asset that produced over $7,000 annually. No repairs ever, and they made almost every payment on time and in full.

After about five years, I was feeling pretty smart. I'd made back almost all of my original investment, and I was still waiting for the day when they would qualify for a loan and take me out for the balance of about $45,000.

That's when the trouble started.

After being uncharacteristically late on a few payments, I reached out to the now-sheepish buyer. "Darryl and I split up. And I moved back to Maryland. I didn't want to miss any payments, so I subleased to a family I trusted. Well, used to trust. They haven't paid me for months. And I can't make any more payments. Please sell it to someone else and pay me whatever you think is fair."

I will spare you the details, but suffice it to say that my renter-buyer was *not at all* qualified to screen tenants. This home was completely trashed. A home that had been nicely rehabbed by me, and meticulously maintained for years by the original renter was now a complete and utter wreck. I sort of understand why they stole all the appliances, but we hadn't forced an eviction or interacted with them at all, so it is somewhat mysterious to me why they went to the extra effort to damage walls, ceilings and the exterior.

I don't know how one family could cause that much damage in a few months. But I know by what was left behind that this drama featured a dog (or *dogs*), a baby (or *babies*), alcohol (or *alcoholics*), a lot of cigarettes, and people who were bent on mass destruction.

I'm just glad these people were never elected to Congress. They would *decimate* our nation! Oh wait... maybe they were.

After numerous repair estimates, I acquiesced to the inevitable: I had the remains of the building hauled off for scrap and sold the lot for $15,500.

So at this point, my wife thinks it's crazy that I used these last two examples. Why would I waste my dear readers' time and three pages of text with irrelevant horror stories that would only make you run away from investing in rental property as fast as you can say "Nightmare on Main Street?"

But that misses the point entirely.

I wrote this book to demonstrate the joys and amazing profitability of fractional multifamily investing. Which necessitates that I tell you what deceptively similar strategies will cause you massive headaches, financial and time losses, and likely not give you the wealth-amassing result you expect. *No matter what the smiling infomercial guy tells you.*

Passively investing in commercial multi-family... with a trustworthy operator/expert asset manager... who utilizes a professional property management firm... is one of the safest, most profitable paths to multi-generational wealth available to the average investor today. The Perfect Investment.

> **Paul's Recipe for *The Perfect Investment*:** Invest in stabilized value-add commercial multifamily properties... through a trustworthy operator/expert asset manager... contracting with a professional property management firm... in a large and growing market.

*But buying single family rentals... or small to mid-sized multifamily properties... and managing them on your own... is virtually **never** a path to the massive wealth available in this asset class.* It is a recipe for headache, a shorter life, and a wasted decade or two. Please don't do it!

So what am I recommending you invest in?

I believe this is the roadmap to multi-generational real estate wealth. We'll be looking at each of these elements in the next few chapters.

Chapter 6 – Your Recipe for Investment Success

Are you old enough to remember The Waltons? Our family gathered around the old Zenith Technicolor TV on most Thursday nights at 8 pm to watch this *mostly* wholesome family show. I say *mostly* because of those two old sisters. At first glance, you'd never guess the Baldwin Sisters were serial felons. Their crime?

The Recipe.

If you don't know what "The Recipe" is, check out the picture of these spinsters along with their recipe at www.wellingscapital.com/therecipe.

If you're still reading this volume, I'm guessing you're looking for a different sort of recipe. Not a recipe to forget your problems and numb your pain. (Unless you've been trying to manage your own small apartments or single family homes.) But a recipe for multi-generational wealth through the channel of commercial multifamily investing.

As a quick reminder, here is **your Recipe for** *The Perfect Investment*:

Invest in *stabilized value-add commercial multifamily* **properties... through a** *trustworthy operator/expert asset manager*...**contracting with a** *professional property management firm*...**in a** *large and growing market.*

I've italicized the terms we will briefly review in this chapter. Note that I'm not necessarily attempting to explain the technical definition of these terms, but the practical explanation for the sake of our discussion. These are the ingredients of your multifamily recipe for success. We will look at them in the order that makes sense...

1. Commercial Multifamily.

A multifamily property is obviously a structure that houses more than one individual or family unit. For example, a lot of folks buy duplexes to live in one half and rent out the other. Or they may buy a four or six-unit complex to manage on their own or through a property manager.

While many people have made a lot of money in this arena, the number of people who can successfully pull this off as a business over the long haul are few and far between. (I discussed this in the previous chapter.)

Commercial multifamily is distinct from *residential multifamily* and *small apartments* in regard to scale. *Residential multifamily* is typically two to four units. It can often be financed though a residential mortgage. Like a home, the value is based on comparable properties.

Small apartments are generally between five and about 70 units. They are financed through a commercial loan, but it is usually a recourse loan. Meaning that banks can come after the owner and his assets in the event of default. These are typically managed by the owner or an off-site property management firm.

A *commercial multifamily* asset is a property that can be managed through a professional property manager. These properties are large enough to profitably employ an on-site staff. The owner would never receive a 3am call about a backed up toilet, and would never face off with a tenant who skipped out on two months rent but remains padlocked inside his apartment.

Commercial multifamily assets can be financed through non-recourse loans, which means the bank cannot pursue the owner in default (with the exceptions of fraud or the introduction of environmental hazards). This is an important distinction from a typical recourse loan.

Commercial multifamily assets are generally valued by income rather than comparables or replacement value (though those two factors can play a role).

As a rule of thumb, for our purposes, the breakpoint between small apartments and commercial multifamily is about 70 units. Institutional investors often want many more units to enter a market. We do, too. Speaking of markets…

2. A large and growing market.

Hopefully I've convinced you to go big. Your second ingredient for success is the market. A lot of things about your investment can be changed. Siding, roofs, landscaping… cabinets, counters and toilets… management, marketing and CPA. But you can never change the location. (Really… just call me Captain Obvious.)

No matter how many things you get right in this business, if you choose the wrong location… the wrong city and neighborhood… you will likely be bound to mediocre results at best. And disastrous results at worst. The flip side is also true. You can get a lot of things wrong, but a great location will cover a multitude of sins. A multitude – but not all.

So what type of city do you want to invest in? And what type of location (submarket) in this city? The full answer is too long for the present treatise. But there are national, regional and specific city trends that should be helpful in this process. For example, people are *generally* relocating from northern cities to the south. There are states whose taxes and laws are friendlier to business growth than others. There are regions whose employment base and infrastructure are conducive to employment and population growth.

A rising tide lifts all boats. A growing population, with growing employment opportunities, increasing wages, low unemployment, low crime, good schools, etc. will likely be a conducive environment for a positive multifamily investment. And if some mistakes are made along the way, as they always are, the "rising tide" will help offset. Unfortunately, a dropping tide, in a lesser city, will sink the best-run property.

This market & submarket analysis is absolutely critical. Unfortunately, it is ignored or botched by many operators. The good news is that if I can help you figure this out so you and your investments are not the victim of their carelessness. It's too important to skim over.

One more note: I just spoke about a growing market. I also said *a large market*. There are a few reasons for this, including the limited swing of cap rate (we'll address that later). Another reason (for commercial multifamily) is that you will want to have a large buyer and seller pool. It's one thing to try to find a buyer for your *duplex* in Chippewa Falls. But it's quite another to locate a buyer who will pay top dollar for your 342-unit complex there. Good luck with that.

Market Analysis Case Study: Asheville, North Carolina

A few years ago, we took a serious look at the Asheville, NC market. We love the Carolinas. They're nearby, and they have many great cities including Charlotte, which is one of America's fastest growing markets.

Asheville has a lot going for it. Asheville's greater metro population is listed at about 438,000, on the low end of the range we would consider. According to the Bureau of Economic Analysis, their population has grown at 1.14% annually, which is 14% faster than the US as a whole over the past ten years. Asheville's net positive domestic migration is reported at a strong 9.9% in the last decade. Their employment growth has averaged an impressive 1.5%, compared to 0.83% for the US. Income has grown at 3.9%, which is higher than any city we've reviewed for acquisitions. Unemployment

(Bureau of Labor Statistics) is a full point better than Charlotte's and 1.5% or so better than the national average, placing them at #104 on the list of 372 cities ranked.

IRR Viewpoint's annual report states that 42.8% of Asheville residents rent, compared to about 36%+ average in the nation. Housing vacancy is high at 2.9% (compared to 2.1% for the US). Apartment vacancy is very low at about 3%. Asheville is ranked 91st out of 226 MSA's ranked by the National Association of Homebuilders for favorable rents compared to home prices. The Office of Federal Housing Enterprise Oversight and the BLS say that 77.4% of Asheville residents can afford to buy a home, compared to 72.1% nationally. (This factor is not favorable for the MSA as a multifamily investment location.)

We also reviewed the number of multifamily building permits (low due to regulatory environment), the Class B inventory (low), Class B vacancy (hard to quantify in a small market but seemed average), historic and projected absorption of new units (positive since moderate building going on), and the apartment transaction volume (very low).

Asheville has an eclectic mix of residents and has a somewhat anti-development mentality. The city is hemmed in by mountains. As a result of these factors, it is difficult to develop new projects. This presents a stronger demand than usual for all grades of apartments. We did, however, consider the possibility that a city like this may one day consider implementing rent controls if this ever becomes a national trend. This would be a big negative for a multifamily property owner.

Though Asheville has a lot going for it, it's size was concerning for us. A few major employers pulling out... and a few new large multifamily projects coming in... and there could be trouble for a multifamily owner.

The other day, about 18 months after our Asheville analysis, I looked up vacancy statistics for Asheville. The average

> **Vacancy** is an important metric when evaluating a market, submarket or property. A few definitions:
>
> **Physical Vacancy.** The percentage of unoccupied units at a given point in time. Calculated as the number of vacant units (including units that are vacant due to time lapse between tenants) divided by the number of total rentable units. In most stabilized multifamily properties, the physical vacancy runs between 1% and 10% or so.
>
> **Economic Vacancy.** Also known as "Vacancy and Credit Loss," this figure includes physical vacancy, but in addition to unoccupied units, it takes into account all of the uncollected potential operating income for an asset. This may include bad debt, marketing concessions to acquire new tenants, units offered at a discount (or free) for staff or security personnel, etc. The economic vacancy at a property is typically a few percentage points higher than the physical vacancy.

apartment vacancy rate is currently running about 10%. This is surprisingly high compared to the rest of the Southeastern US, which is generally averaging closer to 5% in almost every city.

This seemed surprising, so I dialed down a little further. It turns out that the average vacancy in Class B & C apartments built in 1979 or earlier is only about 3%. (When you consider vacancies for units between tenants, and those being remodeled, this number approaches zero vacancy. Similar to 4% US unemployment.) Apartment vacancies for complexes built from the 1980s through 2008 are running almost 7%. And vacancies for apartments built from 2009 to 2016 are averaging a whopping 19%. This includes new complexes that recently opened and are still leasing up at the time of this report (courtesy of Cushman Wakefield).

So what can we learn from this? First, vacancies in a small market can be affected by one or two jolts to the market. A big layoff, or a few new apartment complexes coming online. Second, and more important for our discussion, Asheville's current market bolsters my argument for investing in Class B apartments. Will Asheville's newer Class A apartments eventually fill up? I'm sure they will. But how many millions will be expended on vacant units along the way? How many rent concessions will need to be made? How many disappointed developers will suffer from lower than expected returns along the way?

I don't mean to make a straw-man argument for Class B here, because when I decided to include this case study, I actually hadn't seen the outcome (the current data) yet. (Scout's Honor!) The safety and stability of Class B multifamily, even in a moderately sized market at least at this point in history, is undeniable.

3. A professional property manager.

If location, location, location is your top priority, hiring a professional property manager is in second place. These two factors combined will drive well over half of your investment results.

> Location and your choice of property manager will drive well over half of the results in your multifamily investment. Choose them well.

Your people will make or break your business. Your property management firm is the local face of your company. They are specialists in operating commercial multifamily properties, and the owner/asset managers entrust them with the day-to-day duties of managing the asset.

They hire and manage the staff, manage the budget, screen tenants, collect rent, oversee maintenance and a thousand other things. Don't mess this up. Make sure they're screened well and their references are carefully checked.

So how is your operator doing at checking out their property management firm? You can help them out or check up on them by asking a number of fairly obvious questions like these...

1. How many units do you manage overall?
2. How many units do you manage in this market?
3. Do you own properties in the same market?
4. What software do you use to manage properties? (You want to be sure they don't say "Excel" or some software they created. They should be using nationally recognized software designed for property management.)

There are many more questions you could ask. We have a list of 100, but that's far beyond the scope of this volume.

4. A trustworthy operator.

An operator is more specifically called a Syndicator, or Promoter, or Sponsor, or General Partner. I grew up when *The Godfather* was popular, so I was a bit uncomfortable with being called a *Syndicator* when I first heard the term. A real estate syndicate is a pool of investors who go in together for a common goal, in this case to purchase commercial real estate. It's like high-level crowdfunding long before crowdfunding was cool.

I really like the term Sponsor better than Syndicator, Promoter or Operator, so I will generally use the term *Sponsor,* capitalized through the rest of this book. This term can be synonymous with General Partner in a Limited Partnership, which is another deal structure for the purchase of commercial multifamily assets.

Real estate investors turn to syndicators, aka Sponsors, to get access to deal flow and scale. Individual investors typically don't have the liquid funds to invest in a large-scale commercial property, the type that are often most profitable, so by banding together they can each get a fractional piece of the pie. This is why I refer to this as *Fractional Multifamily Investing.*

Note that this is not a REIT, which is a private or publicly traded corporation that owns and manages real estate holdings. These vehicles are right for some people, but they usually rise and fall with the mood of the market (something I have been running away from). The asset's yield doesn't necessarily equate to a similar ROI for you. And they don't usually provide the surprising tax advantages available to fractional owners of commercial real estate. (We'll talk about that later. You'll be amazed.)

If you plan to invest in fractional commercial real estate ownership, through a syndication model, do yourself a favor and expend the effort to screen your Sponsor carefully. I've written much of this volume to give you a beginner's guide to commercial multifamily investing. Not so you can go out and do it yourself, though you could. I would expect that most readers would use this information to understand the business well enough to carefully screen their Sponsor/asset manager. If you find trustworthy players in these roles, you should be well on your way to building multi-generational wealth in the commercial multifamily investment arena.

The Sponsor is an individual or company charged with finding, underwriting, acquiring and managing the asset. A good Sponsor has a history in real estate, and the ability to perform careful due diligence on assets. They are typically in a position to qualify for commercial debt on the property, which is no small feat as stated earlier.

A good Sponsor has enormous responsibilities in raising and handling finances, finding and screening potential properties, performing hundreds of steps from first offer through closing, and typically managing the asset for years to come. It's a big deal.

One more note… Sponsors have weighty legal requirements to comply with. The Securities and Exchange Commission (SEC) has lengthy rules regarding everything from what they can say to what they can print to who they can talk to and even how long they have known investors before they tell them about a potential opportunity. I'm not a big fan of government regulations, but these regulations are important, and your Sponsor should be keenly aware of them.

The Due Diligence process, or Inspection period, gives the buyer the opportunity to do a deep dive on all financial records, engineering reports, maintenance records, and more. Each lease should be reviewed to assure that all background checks have been done and that all of the appropriate documents are on file. Every single unit should be inspected. Any engineering and soil reports should be reviewed, and every question should be explored. Every roof and HVAC unit should be inspected; the pools, fences, parking lots, retaining walls and grounds should be thoroughly reviewed. No stone should be left unturned. The Sponsor should be deeply involved in this process, and he may contract with the property management firm and others to assist in these activities.

---

5. An expert asset manager.

An asset manager, for our purposes, is usually the same as the Sponsor discussed above. The asset manager is responsible for the ongoing management of the assets purchased in the syndication. This includes the selection and ongoing interface with property managers, lenders, and investors.

The asset manager is charged with making decisions on property upgrades with an eye to bumping up rents and increasing property values and investor equity. The asset manager will manage accounting and finance and (hopefully) order a tax segregation study to accelerate depreciation. The asset manager will work with the property manager to cut costs, improve occupancy and determine budgets for everything from marketing to parking lot restriping. They will suggest additional income streams like revenue-sharing on cable TV and renters' insurance. The asset manager will decide whether to refinance or sell at the end of the loan term.

In short, a good asset manager will maximize return on income and equity on the property for the benefit of all stakeholders. As a passive real estate investor, you should ask your prospective Sponsor a handful of detailed questions about the asset manager on their team. And you should plan to interface with them during the life of your investment.

6. Stabilized properties.

Stabilized refers to a property that is beyond initial lease-up and is already experiencing normal occupancy with rents and income that generally reflect the condition of the property and the supply and demand of the market.

I toured a number of properties in Dallas, Texas last week. One area had about five comparable properties, and they were all between 95 and 99% occupancy. All classified as "stabilized."

Across town, another 600-unit property had less than 400 occupied units. The owner was rehabbing several buildings at a time, and he ran out of money after the first 400 units. These last 200 units have been vacant for years, and they need a lot of work to bring them back online. This is an example of an unstabilized multifamily asset.

There may be many reasons to buy an unstabilized property though.

For one thing, you may be able to get a deal. I mentioned earlier that commercial multifamily properties are valued based on income (we'll discuss this later). The potential income on this 600-unit property is under 2/3rds of what it should be, so it's likely that this off-market property – in a white hot market like Dallas – has *deal* written all over it.

A top-flight asset manager does much more than manage finances, raise rents and upgrade apartments. There are hundreds of ways an asset manager can increase income and value through revenue enhancements and cost savings.

Westdale Asset Management took over a 300-unit property in Atlanta in 2008. They said the property was a water hog, using over 2 million gallons of water per month. With Atlanta's water rates among the highest in the nation, they felt they had to do something.

By spending a quarter million on upgrading their water and sewer system, they began saving $20,000 monthly. This translates to a payback of about one year. That's an ROI of nearly 100%, and an increase to the bottom line of $240,000 annually. But the big payoff comes in the form of value. At a 7% cap rate, the owners just spent $250k to increase the value of the asset by a whopping $3.4 Million! This doesn't include a host of other improvements they implemented. **That's what I call a value-add success story**.

When speaking to the broker, I learned that the owners planned to price the property at a multiple of the net operating income for the 400 operating units (which would equate to about $60,000 per unit) plus about $16,000 each for the other 200 units. These last 200 units would need about $9,000 each to bring them online. So these unoccupied units could theoretically be owned for a total of about $25,000 each (with the headaches of getting them rehabbed and rented). You can see why an investor might want this property.

I know of one investor who would buy this property for cash, do the work in about six months, rent the units, and sell the property for a nice profit in about a year. Quick math: Buy for 400 * $60,000 + 200 * $16,000 = $27,200,000. Repair for 200 * $9,000 = $1,800,000. Add $1,000,000 for other expenses including exteriors, extra marketing and grounds and you have about $30,000,000 in the property.

Assume you sell in one year at the same rate you acquired the stabilized section of the property for: $60,000 * 600 units = $36,000,000. Profit of $6,000,000. Not a bad profit in a year. (I'm not counting any interest expenses, transaction costs, or potential change in supply/demand, etc., but I'm also not counting the increased value per unit based on increased rents, lowering expenses, increased occupancy on the 400 units already in operation, etc., which could be considerable.)

I just spent about a page explaining the virtues of this unstabilized property. So why am I strongly recommending that you invest in *stabilized* properties? There are a few reasons.

First, it's hard to get a traditional lender to jump on board with this plan. Lenders like to play it safe, and they will not provide a traditional loan for a property like this. So this asset will probably need to be acquired with cash or a non-traditional loan (with potentially higher interest.) This is fine, but that is a lot of cash, and you will likely not enjoy the leverage you would get from a safe level of debt.

Secondly, you don't really know what you don't know. (Call me Einstein Jr.) If this was such a great project, why hasn't the current owner done this? Could the owner have pulled in other investors, mezzanine financing or come up with some way to pocket a cool $6 Million on their own? Maybe there are more problems here that aren't readily apparent.

Furthermore, you don't really know if you will be able to lease up the property as easily as you think. This is why banks loan on current income. The last 12 months are more important to them then all of your dreams for what could be.

The final reason I recommend stabilized properties over unstabilized is this: it is consistent with our theme of safety. I blabbered on about not swinging for the fences. Buying the 600-unit property sounds fun and exciting, and it would actually be in my nature to take that project on. But something could go wrong. And I don't want to put my money, my friends' money, or my family's future at stake.

I had lunch with a very successful investment banker &

entrepreneur the other day. I invited Ben, one of our young interns along. He is a recent college grad, hungry to learn all he can. At the end of the meeting, Ben asked the seasoned multi-millionaire for his best piece of advice.

"How old are you?" he asked. Ben is 22. "My best advice is to take all of the risks you can now, while you're young. Before you have a family, a mortgage, kids in school and a ton of other obligations. Take your risks now!"

So here's my bottom line advice about investing in unstabilized properties...

If you're young and have millions to throw around... and you're ok with the chance of losing a bunch... and excited about the chance to make a lot... and you have a knowledgeable team to assist you... and your deal meets the many other criteria I discuss in this book... **then go for it!** I will cheer you on. If I had the cash and knew at 25 what I know now, I probably would have done it.

But if you're perhaps a little older, and/or you're trying to find a safe, careful steady method to grow your wealth, and to build a portfolio that will benefit generations to come... I highly recommend investing in *stabilized* multifamily properties.

I've spent a lot of time on stabilized vs. unstabilized properties, but the implications are broad. Buying unstabilized properties has a similar risk profile to buying small apartments. Or buying in stagnant cities. Or small towns. Or buying single family homes to rent. Or taking other risks. I'm doing what I can to ask you to consider taking all of the risks you can out of the equation. The profits of the low-risk path I'm recommending in this volume are so great that taking an inordinate amount of risk simply makes little sense to me. It makes *The Perfect Investment*...imperfect. In my (mostly) humble opinion.

> **Breakeven Occupancy (BEO).** This fail-safe metric is the occupancy rate at which the cash flow from rents falls to the same level as expenses (operating expenses plus debt service). Typically, today's occupancy rates for stabilized assets are in the 90%+ range. Our team likes to assure that the property would still be profitable if occupancy falls into the 70-75% range (the Breakeven Occupancy). This is *far* below the historical occupancy of well-run assets in solid locations over the past several decades, so this makes us (and our investors and lenders) feel pretty safe.

7. Value-Add Opportunities.

This may be the least familiar term to many readers, but it will make intuitive sense in a moment. Note that the value-add play is not the only way to profitably invest in commercial multifamily. One could invest in new development, unstabilized properties, momentum plays or other opportunities and do very well. But in keeping with our *perfect investment* theme of low risk, stable, careful and predictable, the stabilized value-add play ideally fits the bill.

Though I haven't seen this definition anywhere, the simplest way I can quickly explain the value-add opportunity is: **buying an asset that has a given, known return (Return on Investment - ROI), and meaningfully improving some aspect of the property in a way that the ROI *on the improvements* is much higher than the ROI on the asset as a whole... meaningfully raising the average ROI on the entire project.**

OK, maybe I need to make this simpler...

A buyer of a Value-Add asset recognizes some meaningful shortfall in an asset and spends the money and time to make improvements that raise the rents and net income on the property, making the asset more valuable as a whole.

How about a real example? This would take pages to explain in detail, and you've already had enough of that. This is simplified.

Last Spring, we tried to buy a 130-unit property in the Plaza Midwood neighborhood east of downtown Charlotte. This complex was built in the mid-80s, and it showed. Except for a handful of units, these apartments had barely been remodeled since they were new. The appliances, countertops, lighting, flooring and cabinets were seriously outdated.

The average rent on these apartments was $729, and they were almost completely full. Plaza Midwood is one of those cool areas of town that Millennials are eager to live in.

Developers had built a few new apartment projects nearby, and they were renting for $1,200 or more. At least half a dozen older apartments in the area had been significantly rehabbed, and they rented for $850 to $950 per month on average. These were our "comps" (comparable properties).

We toured several of these properties, and gathered property and rent information. The square footage, amenities, location and size were all similar. The differences were all cosmetic. They had updated flooring, lighting, cabinets (doors and drawer faces), countertops and appliances. They also had nicer landscaping, signs, etc. It was time to analyze.

The rough cost to update these same amenities in our subject property would be $5,500 per unit. A few thousand more if we upgraded to granite countertops and replaced the old cabinets entirely. We believed we could easily raise the average rent by $100, to $829, by making these changes.

We will discuss cap rate later, but to put it simply, for now, it is the rate of return on the property. This can be calculated by dividing the Net Operating Income (NOI) by the cost to purchase the property. The cap rate for a property like this, at this time and this location, was about 7%.

More specifically, the gross annual rents and other income on the property totaled about $1,090,000 (about $8,385 per unit per year). Operating costs were about 50% ($545k or $4,192 per unit annually), leaving a Net Operating Income of $545,000. Dividing the NOI by the cap rate of 7% resulted in a purchase price of about $7.8 Million. (Recall that I mentioned the value of a commercial multifamily is generally based on the income stream, not comparables or replacement cost.) With 130 units, the cost per unit was about $59,900.

Spending $5,500 per unit for upgrades would drive a rent increase of $100 per month ($1,200 annual). This takes the gross annual rent per unit to $9,585 per year with no increase in operating costs. The ROI on the improvements is $1,200 divided by $5,500, almost 22%. This is over three times the ROI (purchase cap rate) on the property (7%), so it creates a net increase in property value. How much?

The new gross income on the property will be about $829 * 125 units (accounts for vacancy) * 12 months = $1,243,500. Subtracting $545,000 in operating expenses leaves an NOI of $698,500. Diving by a 7% cap rate produces a new value of the property of $9.98 million. This is an increase of almost $2.2 million in value, close to $1.5 million net after the cost of upgrades. All things being equal, this will go directly into the owners' collective pockets. And this doesn't include significant cost savings measures we could implement to improve the net income further.

One great way to add value is to increase "Other Income" for an asset. This may include application fees, utility reimbursements, property insurance, pet fees, unreturned deposits, late fees, laundry income, vending machine income, parking fees, cable/internet/ phone services, and more. A great asset manager will look for these opportunities and implement them.

So the value-add is based on the fact that the ROI of the upgrades is much higher than the ROI on the property in general.

It is important to understand that these upgrades may take a few years to implement since they are generally undertaken when tenants move out. It's also key to test these rehabs to assure that they will improve rents as much as your theory.

Asset managers may test different combinations of upgrades to see which produce the most rent growth. Sometimes property managers show a few of the upgraded units to a tenant who has given notice to move out. Often these tenants are willing to pay the additional rent and stay at the property, which is a double bonus since this tenant is retained with no marketing cost. These tenants can be excellent test cases to determine which improvements are most valuable. It is important to always give the majority of the weight to those who vote with their wallets, not just their opinions.

So why would a seller leave this type of value-add opportunity for a buyer? Why wouldn't they do the work and enjoy the increased income and value themselves? There are a number of potential reasons.

A. In the commercial lending world, loans are typically structured as balloon notes, so they have a set date on which they must be paid off. This means the property must be refinanced or sold at a certain time, or the owner chooses pre-payment penalties (if sold too soon) or potential default (by not paying off or refinancing). If the owner decides to sell, he may not have time to make all of these changes. Especially since most of these updates are only done when a unit is vacated.

B. Even if the property is profitable, the owner may be unable or unwilling to provide the capital necessary to undertake these improvements.

C. Remodeling is a hassle, and the owner and/or property manager may not want to undertake it on a large scale.

D. Remodeling can mean down units, which means no

rent, and this is very significant in the year or so before the sale. Why? As we saw a few pages back, the value of the asset is based on the income, and buyers typically look back at least 12 months.

E. A value-add opportunity can generate more interest among buyers. A status quo property, sometimes referred to as a momentum play, can bring a yawn from the buyer community. But when buyers know they can undertake improvements that can give them a nice bump in value, more buyers are willing to bid, which can drive up the price relative to the income.

Given these factors, when a buyer is preparing to sell, they will often remodel a handful of units as a test case. This will prove to the buyers what they could expect if they remodel the balance of the units. This is what many buyers, including our firm, are looking for.

One more note on value-adds. Don't confuse deferred maintenance with a value-add opportunity. A property needing extensive roofs, gutters, landscaping and siding may be less appealing and therefore *possibly* suffer from lower occupancy. But spending a boatload of cash to fix these things will not necessarily provide a predictable increase in rent.

And don't necessarily think that every meaningful upgrade will bump rents. In the hipster Charlotte neighborhood I mentioned, a $1,000 washer/dryer hookup could drive $50 in additional rent (that's a smokin' hot 60% ROI ($50 * 12 = $600 ÷ $1,000 cost). And it could add up to add about a million to the value of the 130-unit complex ($600/yr. * 130 units * 90% occupancy ÷ 7% cap rate.)

But an $8,000 playground would add little value in most residents' minds. I'd advise my asset manager to use the same amount of cash and dirt on a bark-park for little Fifi. (But that theory would need to be tested as well.)

Chapter 7 – Making Millions through Market Selection

My grad school friend and development partner in a successful Midwest multifamily project called me last Saturday to check in. We talked about the business and he commented on his friend, Bill, a sharp 40-something multifamily operator from Denver.

He said, "Bill is proof that you could make a bunch of mistakes in multifamily, but if you get just one thing right, you can make millions. Even if you didn't plan it that way."

Ok Class, what do you think that "one thing" is? Go back to the top criteria for multifamily success from the last chapter. The answer is, of course, location (location, location).

Bill had purchased a number of properties in Denver during the recession. He was able to acquire many under-performing deals, and he made some smart moves to turn them around. But of course he hadn't done everything right. As the recession receded, Denver boomed, and the market for all Denver real estate took off like a rocket. To say the least.

He told me about a residential realtor with 37 buyer clients... and not a home to sell them. Properties are selling within minutes of hitting the market at the time of this writing, and it isn't letting up. My friend told me his son was looking for a small space for a downtown Denver gourmet restaurant and there were no good ones to be found. The poor kid finally relocated to the West Coast.

Prices for Denver multifamily properties have gone crazy. Investors are willing to buy a property with the expectation of only a 5% (or less) annual return (cap rate) – before paying debt service (if applicable). Denver cap rates during the recession were in the 7% range.

Your choice of location will be a significant – likely the most significant – choice you make in selecting a commercial multifamily asset. I can't overstate the importance of this decision.

How to help your Sponsor avoid a mistake that could cost you (and your Sponsor) dearly...

You now have been informed... and warned... about the importance of choosing the right market (and submarket) for your multifamily investment. Unfortunately, many real estate Sponsors aren't aware (or conveniently ignore) this important information. They may choose an investment in their hometown, or one that seems underpriced, or one they heard about on Loopnet (the commercial real estate MLS).

But without undertaking a careful analysis of the market's fundamentals, there is no reason to believe the investment will perform optimally in a good market, or be shielded from difficulties in a poor one.

Don't fall in love!

This is a widely known but easy to make mistake in commercial real estate. You find a nice building, run the numbers and it shows double-digit returns. You become emotionally attached to the deal (even if you won't admit it). You begin to look for all the positives, and you start to overlook or justify the negatives about the property or the location. Everything you turn up that's positive bolsters your opinion, and even the negatives look like exciting opportunities for improvement. In short, you've fallen in love.

"*...a man hears what he wants to hear and disregards the rest.*" -Simon & Garfunkel (The Boxer)

This is true in so much of life, and its applications are all around us. But the successful real estate investor can't afford to do this. You simply must evaluate, with as much objectivity as possible, the market, the submarket and the specific location *before looking at the asset*. It is a fallacy to look at the numbers and other details of a project and ignore the surrounding demographics and surrounding environment that will drive so much of the rise and fall of this asset.

This can be tricky, since apartments are real estate… and so is your home. If you're like most of us, you chose your home partly by falling in love. Don't do this with investment real estate!

Commercial real estate pro Bob Rein said, "Probably the single biggest reason for failure is chasing bad deals. It is very easy to fall in love with the deal or the property that we justify our conclusions regardless of what the numbers tell us. We will stretch for yield or write off red flags in order to justify the decision to invest."

Renowned physicist Richard Feynman said, "The first principle is that you must not fool yourself, and you are the easiest one to fool."

You can be a great asset manager for a great property with a great property manager… in a market where people are leaving, or a submarket where vacancies are high, and you won't achieve great success in this business. You can have a great property in a great market and hire a bad property manager and that's another way to fail.

> *"The market you choose to work in… and the property manager you choose to work with… will drive 70% of your success in this business."* **– Kieran Donohue, 37ᵗʰ Parallel Properties**

Can you still make money in markets like my old hometown of Detroit? Absolutely. But there are only so many hours in a day, and in keeping with our theme of low risk and predictable returns, doesn't it make more sense to play in markets that provide a proven context for success?

Start by selecting your market well.

We utilize a list of almost two-dozen metrics that allow us to analyze a market in just a few hours. I am indebted to Dan Chamberlain of Multifamily Partner Program Properties for assembling the components of our analysis. You can visit their website to learn more at www.37parallel.com.

These statistics are typically available by knowing where to look online. Your Sponsor should have resources to evaluate these types of factors. They include metrics like:

➤ Population and Population Growth
➤ Employment and Income Growth
➤ Unemployment
➤ Rental Vacancy Rates
➤ Planned Multifamily Construction (building permits)

If you're planning to make an investment, I recommend that you assure your Sponsor has carefully evaluated these types of factors for the market(s) that you're counting on to help you grow your multi-generational investment portfolio. You may save yourself a lot of heartache… help your Sponsor out… and look super-smart along the way. And isn't that what's most important – really?

> "You ought to be able to explain why you're taking the job you're taking, why you're making the investment you're making, or whatever it may be. And if it can't stand applying pencil to paper, you'd better think it through some more. And if you can't write an intelligent answer to those questions, don't do it."
> **– Warren Buffett**

Selecting Your Submarket

Now we're going to look at how to select a great submarket.

More specifically, we'll be discussing how to be sure the submarket for the asset you're considering will support your investment goals. As stated earlier, regardless of what you do to your asset, no matter how pretty or well run, you can't pick it up and move it. So the importance of the specific location cannot be overstated.

There are two categories of analysis that need to be undertaken in reviewing a neighborhood. (This chapter is not divided into these categories since the topics here are helpful for both types of analysis.) The first is **armchair analysis**. This is the type you can do from the comfort of your home, in your PJs if you wish. These are the demographics that provide a screen for what you will expect to see when you hit the ground, or even if you should hit the ground. New tools have made this process easier than the previous generation could have ever dreamed, and it will be helpful if you, as a passive investor in particular, take advantage of these.

The second category of analysis is your **on-the-ground analysis**. Before making an offer on a property, the Sponsor should obviously spend a lot of time seeing the area and the asset in person – which goes without saying. You may also want to go along as well.

The Major Issues

The major issues when reviewing an MSA relate to population, jobs and income. For a neighborhood, the key factors relate to crime, schools, shopping and jobs. Crime and schools are two of the major draws and detractors for renters moving into your neighborhood. It is important to review these factors relative to the city and state as opposed to the nation. Convenience to transportation is also important, but this is usually another Goldilocks situation… you want convenience, but you don't necessarily want to be right in front of mass transit.

When I'm presented with a deal, assuming I already like the MSA, I glance at the age and the size of the asset to assure it fits our parameters. Then I immediately check it out on Google (or you may choose Bing) Maps to see where it fits within the market. I don't bother reading all the sales literature from the broker. I don't bother with the numbers. I start by looking at the neighborhood. Because there's no deal that I want to pursue, for my investors or myself, in a crummy neighborhood.

As a former residential investor, I was taught that every house had some value. But when stewarding my investors' capital and signing my name on a large loan, there are many "good" deals that I don't want any part of. You may see it differently.

Assuming I already have at least a general understanding of the market as a whole, I use the Google Maps aerial view to see where this asset is in relation to beltways, shopping, industrial, downtown, schools, airports and suburbs.

After looking over the submarket, drag the little yellow guy down from the upper right screen corner and get a *brief* street view. There are other important factors to consider, so I recommend only doing a quick tour up and down several blocks for now.

Before thinking too deeply about what you see on the street view, check the image date on the bottom right to see when these photos were actually taken. A lot can change, especially in urban areas in large MSAs, so if the images are several years old, be sure to correlate what you see with other information you're gathering.

After checking Google Maps, you can dig into more information about the neighborhood using a variety of online tools. (Again, your Sponsor should be doing all of this.) We look at schools, crime, incomes, housing costs and trends, walkability and much more.

One caution. A number of times we've been misled by this

data in areas that are on a dramatic upswing. We screened out a property in Winston-Salem once based solely on the crime scores, but we later learned that these scores did not reflect the latest situation on the ground there. Make sure to use a cross-section of the tools, maps and other data available to you.

Another time we hit the ground in Charlotte in a neighborhood that looked sketchy online. Not only on an older image on Google Maps, but on crime score and school sites as well. We first noticed that it had perhaps the nicest Harris Teeter grocery store we had ever seen. And many newly revamped homes and retail stores.

We finally approached a store manager who was chatting with a policeman on the sidewalk outside his lovely store. He explained that the area had undergone a dramatic overhaul in the past few years, and he believed the map and statistics had not caught up with the reality of the situation there. So statistics do lie, but this was one case where they lied in a different way than I usually think of!

Speaking of stores, you should also look at the types of stores in the submarket. The type of chains in the area should help define the demographics of the people nearby. So if there is a Whole Foods nearby, you can bet their demographers believe there are fairly affluent people in the area. Contrast to a Food Lion. Food Lion isn't necessarily bad for your project… your tenants may actually shop at Food Lion more often than Whole Foods. We are just getting a precise picture of the area remotely.

Apartment Publication Tools

Your Sponsor should take some time perusing online apartment sites in the submarket. These tools will provide an idea of the competition for the asset you're considering. If the broker is telling you these apartments rent below the market, perusing these listings for rents on nearby apartments of similar age, size and amenities should give you an idea if he's telling you the truth.

Google Maps or Google Earth – Time for a Deeper Dive

Once you've briefly screened the asset using these tools, I recommend doing a much more thorough virtual tour through the neighborhood. Using the street view in Google Maps or Google Earth will give you a wonderful tour, and possibly save you airline expenses and hours of driving. (Of course the Sponsor will need to spend a lot of time on the ground if making an offer on the property. But I'm referring to initial screening by the Sponsor, or the screening you will do as a passive investor.)

Here is a short list of things we look examine in the area. Your sponsor will be looking at these things as well.

➤ Residential
➤ Retail
➤ Employers
➤ Entertainment
➤ Schools
➤ Health Care

A few final thoughts on submarkets

Your Sponsor will never have the manpower or the funding to hire demographers like Trader Joe's, Starbucks or Kroger. The great news is that they don't have to. By locating near quality businesses like these (and dozens of others), you can be pretty sure you're in a good location to grow your investment portfolio.

As I write this, we are considering the purchase of a property in Fort Mill, SC. This is a particularly attractive opportunity because this formerly sleepy town is only 25 minutes from booming downtown Charlotte, it has lower South Carolina taxes, but perhaps most importantly, it boasts one of South Carolina's top school districts. Some people will pay higher rent to get into this district. Think carefully about the demographic trends in an area. Where they are today, and where they're moving. Fort Mill didn't seem like a place I'd want to invest a decade ago. A lot can change in ten years.

Note that drug stores, even national chains, are not necessarily a bonus for an area since these facilities locate based on traffic count more than demographics in general. Walgreen's and CVS stores are located in the midst of million dollar neighborhoods... and ghettoes.

One of the commercial properties I helped develop and still co-own is right next door to a new medical center and across the street from a parcel with a planned WalMart. Walking distance to both. This is a great source of traffic, a benefit to the tenants, and a great source of nearby jobs to attract tenants.

While researching for this book, I came across a great article by Ryan Severino in Multifamily Executive Magazine. Ryan is senior economist and director of research at real estate and analysis firm Reis, based in New York. He is also an adjunct professor at Columbia University and NYU. I contacted Ryan and he was kind enough to give me permission to reprint the article in its entirety here.

Class B Offers Choice Investments
They may not be the prettiest of properties, but B and C developments can yield attractive returns.
By Ryan Severino

Would you rather have a B or a C than an A? Not likely in academics. Probably not likely in restaurant sanitation grades either. But how about in apartment investing?

While B and C properties are often not the most aesthetically pleasing, there are compelling reasons why they present excellent investment opportunities, possibly even better than does Class A, for the next few years.

Affordability

Let's start with the most obvious reason B and C properties perform well—affordability, or the lack thereof.

Most households living in B/C apartments are doing so out of necessity, not preference. If they could afford something better, they'd likely choose it. However, with median real household income falling over the past two decades, many households have limited ability to spend on goods and services, especially housing. This situation relegates them to B/C apartments and essentially excludes these households from purchasing a home. That's especially true these days, with residential mortgage underwriting standards remaining so stringent. Indeed, it's tremendously difficult for many households to obtain a mortgage, even an FHA loan. Although FHA loans are ideal for lower-income households, many of these households have impaired credit that puts even this option out of reach.

The "A" Team

What about the potential for moving up into a Class A apartment? It doesn't require the same stringent under-writing that a mortgage does. Moreover, if you look out at the swelling construction pipeline, the overwhelming majority of new properties being developed are Class A. Could the intense competition between Class A prop-erties cause rents to fall enough that they'd be affordable for Class B or C residents?

As I've heard stated by a number of individuals over the past year, "Yesterday's Class A is today's Class B!" Yet, this, also, is a highly unlikely scenario. While the pipeline is robust for Class A, the difference between A and B/C rents is too large to be narrowed enough to put the A rents within reach of most Class B/C renters. For example, the national Class A rent premium over Class B/C is an astonishing 41%. The narrowest margin is in Syracuse, N.Y., at 29%, and the widest is in Westch-ester, N.Y., at 69%.

Lack of Competition

With the majority of the pipeline focused on Class A, there's little to no competition from new Class B or C apartments. In fact, in recent years, Class B/C inventory has actually been declining, due to conversions, demolitions, etc., which are not adequately being replaced by either new construction or Class A properties sliding down into the B/C category. This presents an ample opportunity for Class B/C rent growth to accelerate.

Although apartment rent growth is surely constrained by income growth, household incomes are projected to keep growing, which will enable B/C landlords to continue to increase rents. Meanwhile, Class A rent growth will slow and compress toward the inflation rate, weighed down by all the new competition in the market. Additionally, the lack of new competition in the B/C space will continue to put downward pressure on an already incredibly low vacancy rate.

The Class B/C vacancy rate is now 220 basis points lower than Class A's. This wasn't always the case, but the hundreds of thousands of new Class A units that have been added over the past few years have pushed Class A vacancy well above Class B/C's. Therefore, it's highly likely that NOI growth for Class B/C properties will exceed that for Class A properties over the medium term.

Investment Outlook

Beyond the fundamentals, there's also a capital markets argument for B/C investment. Class B/C properties typically trade at a discount to Class A properties. On the cap rate side, the discount is currently equivalent to about 100 basis points. And while higher cap rates usually reflect greater risk or worse NOI growth prospects, that doesn't look to be the case now.

Obviously, each property will differ, but from a macro perspective, at the moment there appear to be more risks associated with Class A than with B/C, and Class A is likely to have slower NOI growth than Class B/C.

A higher cap rate and faster NOI growth? Looks like B/C will be making the grade while Class A is sent to detention.

Ryan Severino is senior economist and director of research at real estate and analysis firm Reis, based in New York. He is also an adjunct professor at Columbia University and NYU. Reprinted in its entirety with permission of the author.

www.multifamilyexecutive.com/business-finance/class-b-offers-choice-investments_o (Accessed August 7, 2016)

We've spent a lot of time on market and submarket. It has probably become apparent to you how critical this is in selecting your asset. Now it's time to dive more deeply into the numbers and reasons that make commercial multifamily The Perfect Investment.

Chapter 8 – The Mechanics of Multifamily

So I've made the case that commercial multifamily investing has compelling demographic, financial and operational drivers that have caused many investors to believe it is indeed The Perfect Investment. The return to risk profile is surprisingly strong.

Check out this graphic from Thomson Reuters:

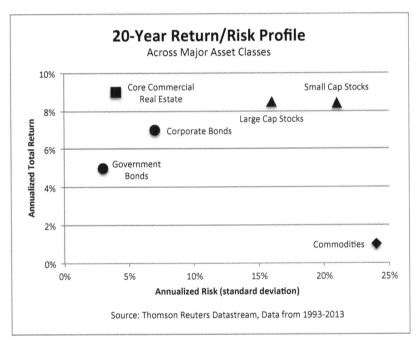

If you have invested in any of the asset classes in this graph... or if you have been burned by swinging for the fence and missing a few times... then this graph alone should be enough to get your attention.

Take a close look. Note that core commercial real estate has by far the best risk-adjusted returns of the major asset classes. This analysis applies to all core commercial real estate, including office, retail, manufacturing space, storage, and multifamily.

Here's why I've invested my life and my finances and my future in multifamily...

Think about the demographic factors I laid out in Chapter 4. The long-term impact of the retiring baby boomer generation. The Millennial generation's enduring propensity to rent. And the ever-expanding influence from a growing immigrant population.

Then consider the risk profile of multifamily compared to single family through the last recession and now. Recall that the Freddie Mac delinquency rate was 90% lower for multifamily during the recession, and it was 98% lower by 2015.

I consider this sufficient evidence to select commercial multifamily as the ideal investment among the commercial asset classes. (Some wise guy even called it The Perfect Investment!)

Now let's take a look at the Sharpe Ratio.

The Sharpe Ratio is a measurement of the risk-adjusted return for investments. The goal, of course, is to get the highest return per "unit of risk." Check out this graph showing the Sharpe Ratios of various asset classes:

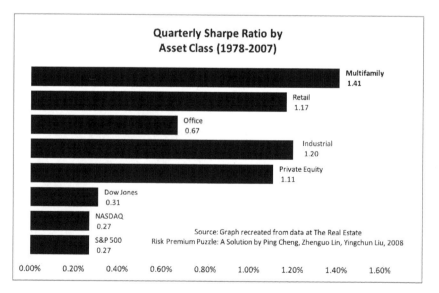

Quarterly Sharpe Ratio by Asset Class (1978-2007)

Multifamily 1.41
Retail 1.17
Office 0.67
Industrial 1.20
Private Equity 1.11
Dow Jones 0.31
NASDAQ 0.27
S&P 500 0.27

Source: Graph recreated from data at The Real Estate Risk Premium Puzzle: A Solution by Ping Cheng, Zhenguo Lin, Yingchun Liu, 2008

The multifamily Sharpe Ratio is 4.6 times better than the Dow Jones index, 1.3 times better than private equity, and almost 1.4 times better than the average of the other three commercial asset classes for the period analyzed.
Honestly, it was information like that contained in these last two graphs that caused me to wake up to the power of the multifamily sector, and to eventually throw my hat fully in this ring.

"The apartment sector recovered quickly from the last recession. The period between 2010 and 2012 was one of the best on record for the industry in terms of net operating income growth. This growth was fueled by big gains in both occupancy and rent prices and aided by very limited new supply."
– Jay Parsons, Director, MPF Research.
www.americanbanker.com/bankthink/is-multifamily-housing-the-next-lending-bubble-1069988-1.html (Accessed November, 20, 2015)

As we discussed before, the foreclosure rate of multifamily assets in the Great Recession was under one percent. (Compare this to the non-performance rate of first liens for single family homes held by banks, which peaked at over 9% in 2010.) When you factor out the highly volatile sand states of Florida, Nevada, Arizona and California, the foreclosure rate of multifamily properties was a fraction of that. Zeroing in on assets in solid, low-crime sub-markets, run by a professional property manager drops the rate to close to zero.

I met with Micah Spruill for dinner last night at my favorite Asian restaurant. Micah is an up-and-coming Atlanta investment strategist, and he has a critical eye to see through lying statistics. (You know the type of stats I'm talking about.)

I showed Micah a graph contrasting average renter income and rents through the Great Recession. His reaction surprised me. He said, "Start your next investor presentation off with this graph. Any smart investor should see this and cut the meeting short in less than five minutes. And write you a check on the spot!" Check out this graph...

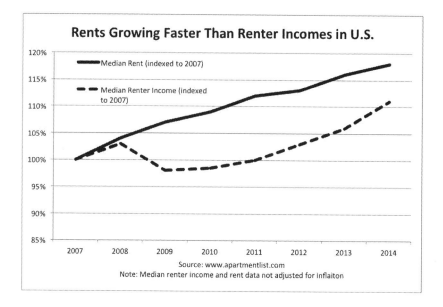

Do you see how powerful this is? While incomes (along with single family home prices) dropped like a rock during the recession, **rents continued to rise**. This graph, or actually the data behind it, is yet another reason I went out on a limb to label carefully procured and professionally managed commercial multifamily *The Perfect Investment*.

Rent vs. Income: The View Over Half-a-Century

I was feeling pretty good about the rent versus income picture from 2007 to 2014. Here's a brief window into my inner-brain (is there an outer-brain?): "This really is a recession-resistant investment. Perhaps the best I've ever seen. But I'm looking for an investment that will be safe and stable and profitable for the rest of my life, and hopefully, during my children's lifespan as well."

Seasoned commercial real estate investor Scott Lawlor was hurt like most others in the 2008 downturn. Since 2012, he has amassed over $1 billion in investor capital and purchased 37 multifamily assets totaling over 12,000 doors. Impressive.

Scott said, "Apartments, as far as we can tell, are the only property with meaningful structural tailwinds that have nothing to do with next quarter's GDP growth. Whether it's a shift in home-ownership patterns in the U.S. or the demographic wave coming through the pipeline, there are half a dozen bullet points driving apartment demand that have nothing to do with next quarter's GDP."

www.multifamilyexecutive.com/business-finance/leadership/lawlor-builds-an-institutional-platform-for-high-net-worth-investors (Accessed July 19, 2016)

A month or two later, I stumbled across a nearly identical graph, from a related but stronger source, with a view across several decades. Here it is…

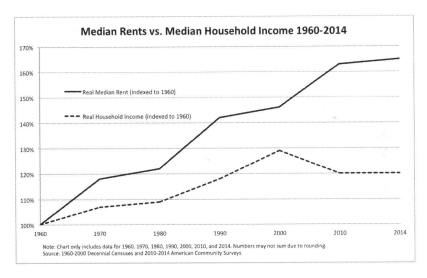

This picture says it all. What more is there to say?

How is Return Derived?

"So Paul," I hear some of you asking, "you are trumpeting the marvelous returns derived through the multifamily sector. How are these returns derived?"

I'm glad you asked.

Return on Investment is derived from four components. CAPT for short. Not a great acronym, but better than *CATP*. (Say it out loud if you didn't get it.)

C = Cash Return
A = Appreciation
P = Principal Paydown
T = Tax Benefits

CAPT 1 = C: Cash Return

This is pretty self-evident. This return is derived from the free cash flow of the property. As an investor in commercial multi-family, it is likely that your cash returns will be higher – much higher – than the taxable income on your K-1. We'll get into that more in the tax chapter.

Of course this will vary widely, but for the purpose of this book, here's a very rough estimate on how your cash returns could shake out based on $100 of gross operating income…

Gross Income	$100
Less Operating Expenses	$50
Net Income	**$50**
Less Capital Reserves	$4
Less Loan Principal & Interest	$26
Less Asset Management Fee	$4
Free Cash Flow	**$16**

Under a typical scenario where the Gross Income is about 20% of the asset value, leveraged at about 67%, this would translate to a cash-on-cash return of about 9 to 10%.

Typical cash-on-cash returns for stabilized Class-B Value-

Add assets are between 5% and 7% early on, and up to about 12% later in the ownership period. *But that's not all you get...*

Operating Expenses are the sum of all expenses required to operate a multifamily asset. These are reported in a fairly standard manner in the industry, and they typically total between 40% and 60% of the Gross Operating Income. Operating Expenses typically include repairs, maintenance, turnover (preparing units for a new tenant), grounds, property management fees, salaries and wages, administrative, promotional/advertising, property taxes, and insurance.

CAPT 2 = A: Appreciation

As we discussed earlier, the value of a stabilized commercial multifamily asset is generally the Net Operating Income (NOI) divided by the Cap Rate. While both of these numbers are subject to some market forces beyond the operator/investor's control, there are many factors that are controllable through careful planning and execution. This is where I think Class B, Value-Add shines as a sub-class of the Multifamily sector.

Since appreciation is a function of both NOI and Cap Rate, I will be discussing both in detail below.

Improving Net Operating Income is based on increasing rental income and other income while maintaining or decreasing operating costs. We discussed the fact that Value-Add properties provide an opportunity for the new owner to achieve a disproportionately high ROI on capital and management improvements made to the property. This may be derived from a long list of factors, but a few examples include **increasing rents**, occupancy and other income by:

➤ Improving the property's interior and exterior appearance and functionality.

➤ Increasing the effectiveness of marketing.
➤ Adding (or upgrading) valuable features such as dog parks, swimming pools, rentable carports, exercise facilities and appliances (like washers and dryers in units).
➤ Adding or improving revenue centers like bulk cable, Internet and phone services, pet fees, renter insurance, laundry facilities and more.
➤ Passing back utility costs previously absorbed by owners (electricity, water/sewer, gas, Wi-Fi, pest control, and trash pickup).

Examples: A Fort Worth acquisition target I reviewed this week had individual electric meters, but the owner paid the water/sewer, gas, pest control and trash. It would cost a few hundred dollars per unit to install meters for water and sewer, but the new owner could pass over $400 per unit annually back to residents by taking this action. (Note over 100% ROI!) In checking around the submarket, we learned that about three out of every four similar properties billed these costs back to tenants, so it was safe to believe this could be done without major disruption to the property's tenant marketability. Chalk up about $150,000 annually on the "Other Income" line.

Before focusing in on Class B Value-Add properties, my partner and I developed and operated a new multifamily asset in the Midwest a number of years ago. When surveying the market, we learned that almost all of the competition had only central laundry facilities or no laundry available at all. By designing each unit with a washer and dryer, we were able to increase rents by at least $75/month, and occupancy was better as well. This was nearly a 100% ROI as well.

Net Operating Income may also be improved by **reducing costs**. A good asset manager and property manager will have dozens of ways to achieve this. Examples of expense categories to manage include:

> ➤ Payroll and benefits
> ➤ Property Taxes
> ➤ Insurance
> ➤ Utilities
> ➤ Administration and management expenses
> ➤ Repairs, maintenance and unit turnover
> ➤ Eliminating ineffective marketing expenditures

Examples: I recently reviewed a potential acquisition in North Carolina. In examining the trailing twelve-month financials (referred to as a T-12), many items stood out. This property had become a cash cow for the owner, and it wasn't clear that he was paying attention to costs. For example, they were giving a free unit to a police officer who lived in the complex, and paying him to occasionally patrol the property. Annual tab: $35,000. The complex was in a previously seedy area that had gone through a major transformation. I think the officer was a holdover from a previous era. This could be eliminated.

Then there was the Charlotte property whose owner was a buddy with the owner of the property management firm. The property management firm had helped the owner design and develop the project in the 80's, and the owner was finally retiring. The property management firm charged a whopping 12.5%. Three to five percent is normal. An opportunity to save $80,000.

It's easy to imagine the four scenarios (and *many* more) above as part of a value-add opportunity at one asset. How would this affect appreciation? More than you might guess.

1. Utility bill-back to tenants: $150,000 Income
2. Add washer/dryers: $81,225 Income
3. Eliminate security officer: $35,000 Savings
4. Change property management co.: $80,000 Savings

So these four changes would add about $346,225 to the annual net income (NOI) of our theoretical multifamily property. At a 7% cap rate, these changes alone would result in an **increased property value to the property of $346,225 ÷ 7% = $4.9 million.**

So on a property purchased at $40 million, the owner who made these four changes just took steps leading to appreciation of over 10% of its value. Of course these efforts would require capital and time to implement and could affect occupancy in some cases, but this is a rough estimation for the purpose of explanation.

What is the effect of 10% appreciation for investors with (say) 2:1 leverage (66.6% LTV debt) on their cash invested? Again, there are other factors involved, but it should be about 3x (3 x 10% = **30% ROI**). This is before rent growth and dozens of other strategies that could increase the asset's income and value.

We've discussed the role of income and expenses in driving appreciation. One more category that deserves mention is **rentability**. This is a subjective category that is harder to quantify, but nonetheless important. Rentability may not directly result in the opportunity to raise rents; it may not result in any cost savings; but it is likely to increase occupancy and tenant retention, and therefore the overall income and value of the property.

Improving rentability can often be achieved by bringing in a great property management team. It can be as simple as hiring a great property manager who possesses stellar character. Character that cannot be taught or trained but is a function of who the person is.

Some of the factors driving increased rentability include:

➤ Professionalism
➤ Dependability/Follow-through
➤ Convenience

➤ Aesthetics
➤ Community
➤ Tenant Customer Service

What goes up... must come down.
It should be noted that value-add and other improvements to income and asset value always play an important role in driving investor returns. They are especially important in an environment of cap rate expansion. In a declining economy, the cap rate may expand by a percent or even two. The changes your asset management team makes to drive improved rents and occupancy, decrease costs, increase other income, etc., will effectively offset the potential decrease in value due to cap rate expansion.

This expansion and contraction is just a fact of life for commercial real estate. This fact underscores the importance of investing with a skilled and ethical Sponsor who chooses a large and stable market and only purchases assets with multiple opportunities to increase rents, decrease costs and improve occupancy.

As I said, I believe it is principally a function of hiring the right people, particularly the Property Manager, who will pick his or her team. But I have found an organization that can really help Property Managers achieve their goals. It's called ApartmentLife.org. This organization sends a small team (often a married couple) onsite to live at a property. You can check them out if you have an interest in turning your apartment complex into a true caring, connected community.

Now that we've talked a lot about the role of NOI in driving appreciation, let's move on to Cap Rate.

Your cap rate (capitalization rate) represents the market's evaluation of your unleveraged yield for that asset class in that market. Integra Realty Resources (www.IRR.com) states that the cap rate is driven by these seven factors:

1. Supply and Demand.

2. Property Income Growth.
3. Local economy, Job Growth, Unemployment
4. National Economic Conditions/GDP Growth.
5. Interest Rates.
6. Availability of Financing.
7. Risk Premium of Private Real Estate.

Our team generally likes to work in markets where cap rates vary from 6.5% to 8.5%. Cap rates on the lower end of the spectrum (higher-priced asset purchases) can be managed by aggressive rent growth in the first few years and through interest-only loans (typically available for up to three to five years).

MSAs with very low cap rates (*expensive!*) such as New York, San Francisco and Chicago will usually not cash flow during the first few years of the investment. Institutional investors like insurance companies and REITs can handle this type of return profile because they realize it will translate to very steady yields in later years. Lower cap rate markets are expensive, but typically more stable. Buyers in these realms are willing to pay a premium for this predictability.

Low cap rates do not necessarily speak to the health of the market as much as they do the stability. For the typical investor, these ultra-low cap rate markets don't make as much sense as moderate rate markets.

What about high cap rate markets? Should you celebrate the opportunity to buy in a 9% cap market? Maybe. But not necessarily. These markets can experience the widest swings in value... opposite the ultra-low markets.

Of course it is possible to get a higher cap rate (lower price) on an individual asset based on a number of risk factors. Earlier we discussed an unstabilized asset in Dallas that can be purchased for a cap rate that could swing wildly to the good based on the asset manager's ability to turn the property around quickly.

Let's take a second to see what this kind of cap rate means to investors. A 250-unit property with a net operating income of $1.2 million in 7% cap rate economy is valued at about $17.1 million ($1.2M÷7%). That same property at the same net income will be valued at $21.8 million if cap rates tighten to 5.5%. Even if this owner did nothing to improve his property and income, the value went up substantially. (Of course investing in value-add properties means your operator will be taking aggressive actions to improve the property, the rents and the net income – regardless of the market. The value-adds can sometimes more than compensate for a negative move in cap rate.)

This change in value was contingent on the change in the economy, but this will be a similar move for many markets. The strength of this change was largely based on the particulars in this market. Note that the first three of the seven cap rate factors (above) are mostly localized in nature, while the last four are more national in scope.

In addition to seeing positive changes in good economies, markets with strong fundamentals are often protected from significant drops in poor markets. Take New York. Limited supply, astronomical costs to build and own, and an enormous renter pool have been true of this market for most of the last century (or more). The cap rate and property values there are more insulated than many other locations.

CAPT 3 = P: Principal Paydown

This is pretty simple, and it may not even sound like it should be part of the return. But it is cash that could have been distributed to the investors but is used to increase in equity, so it is certainly part of the return. It consists of the regular paydown of your mortgage balance as part of your monthly debt payments. You won't get rich overnight, but your tenants pay down your mortgage while you sleep, and you do nothing special to achieve this benefit.

This increase in equity typically amounts to a 2% to 4% return annually. As an investor, you won't see any benefit from this in your quarterly distribution, but you will experience this benefit at the time of debt refinance or the sale of the property.

Principle Paydown is a legitimate part of your return because the money spent to pay down the mortgage is cash returns that owner-investors are foregoing year-in-and-out. If there were no paydown, as in the first few years of an interest-only product, this cash would go straight to the distributable cash bucket to be enjoyed by investors.

My business partner owns a small commercial property in Southwest Virginia. He bought this property a number of years back for $2,750,000. It recently appraised at $3.2 million, and he has been paying down the mortgage while it has grown in value.

The current mortgage balance is $1,713,000, so his equity in the asset has grown almost $1.5 million. This growth is based on both appreciation and principal paydown. This could be viewed as lazy equity (I'll cover this more later...equity that is making a lower ROI than it could be). If he refinances, he could potentially take out about three-quarters of a million that he could invest elsewhere for a higher return. He should probably do so, especially in the current low rate environment.

We recently reviewed a Dallas property with 586 units. The estimated (whisper) price was about $55k per unit – $32,500,000 total. We would have financed $24,375,000 and invested $8,125,000 in cash. A 10-year commercial loan with a 30-year amortization schedule.

Principal paydown started at 2.7% (of the total equity) for full year one, and it progressed up to 4.1% by year 10. That was about $379k in year one, progressing up to nearly $579k in year ten. A total paydown and increased equity of $4.7

million in ten years. This is a cumulative ROI (Return on Investment) of $4.7M ÷ $8.125M = 57.8%. A nice addition to the strong cash-on-cash returns and capital appreciation for this asset.

Picky, picky, picky...

A multifamily buyer/owner/operator reviews dozens of deals before choosing one to make an offer on, and typically makes many offers to get one acquisition. Like most others, this Dallas deal was one of many that did not make the cut. There were quite a few competitors willing to pay more, and we decided not to play.

Be sure your multifamily Syndicator is *extremely* picky. Not only on market, but also on the location, the asset and the returns they demand. *And everything else.* This is nothing like finding houses to flip. That takes diligence and many offers, but this is a whole different level.

This is the unfortunate side effect of being in a business with the powerful demographics we discussed before. The trends are clear and the information is easily verifiable. There are billions of dollars from all over the world chasing these deals, and every seller with a good asset knows what they have.

CAPT 4 = T: Tax Benefits

"If the American public knew how little we are taxed, we'd have a revolt on our hands!" So quoted a friend of mine before he launched into an explanation of how he and his investors could parlay $20 million cash into a $210 million portfolio over two decades... pocket $131 million along the way... and pay virtually no taxes. All legal and ethical.

This subject is so important that I've dedicated the entire next chapter to covering it in detail. Read on...

Chapter 9 – Fodder for a Tax Revolt

"If the American public knew how little we are taxed, we'd have a revolt on our hands!"

This California friend and fellow multifamily investor was right. It's really true. And it's yet another reason that, after a multi-faceted career in a variety of entrepreneurial ventures, I have thrown my efforts completely into the multifamily investment ring.

I had only been in the multifamily world for a few years when this friend showed me how he could take $20 million of an investor's money and leverage it to produce $210 million in multifamily assets over 20 years. Throwing off a healthy $131 million in cash flow (to the investor) from years 11 through 20.

That seemed unbelievable...but he had math to prove it.

Then he really amazed me. "How much do you think that investor might pay in taxes over that 20-year period?" he asked. "There's no guarantee, since everyone's situation is different, but I can see how he could pay as little as a few hundred thousand dollars."

Wait. A few hundred thousand dollars tax...on $131 million in free cash flow?

Like I said, some investors got into multifamily investing (and other commercial investing) long before the big demographic shift... for the tax benefits alone.

Expected Disclaimer

Before I proceed, I need to make a few things crystal clear:

1. I am not a CPA or tax professional. I cannot speak to your specific tax situation, and I cannot tell you if all – or any – of

these tax-advantaged strategies will work for you.

> If you take $1.00 and double it [daily] tax-free for 20 days it's worth $1,048,576 (over a million dollars). Take that same $1.00, taxed [every day] at 30%, it will be worth only about $40,640 — A LOSS of a MILLION DOLLARS! Why is this so? Because with tax-free compounding, earnings accumulate not only on the principal amount of money but also accumulate on the tax-free earnings as well. ("Earnings on Earnings".) Thus compounding combines earning power on principal and earning power on interest. Compounding has been called the "8th wonder of the world", a "miracle". Compounding money at high rates of tax-free return is a definite advantage of real estate, especially with a great tax plan.
> *www.blog.ctreia.com/11-powerful-tax-strategies-for-real-estate-investors/ (Accessed November 7, 2015)*

2. Furthermore, I can't verify the accuracy of the information in this chapter. I, and many investors across the nation, utilize these tax benefits year-in and year-out. But that doesn't mean we all have an intricate knowledge of the mechanics behind them. I don't have to understand how the Internet really works to enjoy its benefits. Same here. You and I don't have to study the details of these tax strategies to enjoy their benefits. I hired a professional Tax Strategist several years ago, when my partner and I were building a Hyatt hotel. He and my CPA know the mechanics. So I can focus on other things. My goal in this chapter is not to give you the mechanics behind the curtain, but to continue our conversation of multifamily topics in layman's terms. (This is why I often say "probably" or "likely" in the rest of this chapter. I think I'm likely often right on most of the items… probably most of the time.)

3. Since this book was researched and published at a given point in time, it is obviously possible that the codes and interpretations and rulings affecting these topics may have changed by the time you read this. Another reason to check

with your own tax strategist or accountant.

So what are these amazing tax benefits?

Direct Investment

When you invest in stocks or bonds, including a REIT (real estate investment trust), you are investing in a corporation. An entity that owns things and makes profits.

If you work with the right Sponsor, you should be able to invest directly in commercial real estate. You will be a fractional owner of the property you are investing in, through a limited partnership, a single-use LLC or other entity established just for the ownership of that property.

This is important, because it positions you to take advantage of the other tax benefits of this profitable asset class.

Hire a Tax Strategist

Ed, a friend and fellow multifamily investor, told me the story of why he hired a tax strategist. As a real estate investor and real estate broker, Ed made a lot of profit over a lot of years. And he had a whopping tax bill to prove it.

He once read an article about a surprising tax-savings tip. He met with his CPA to share it, and the CPA agreed that it was a great idea, and that they should start that right away. And maybe even re-file for a few years to capture some of these benefits.

Ed, a bit irritated, pressed his accountant a little further: "Why didn't you tell me about this before?" His CPA answered (to this effect): "You pay me to do your taxes and oversee your bookkeeping. You don't pay me to be a tax strategist. I just take what you give me and file your returns. There are probably dozens of ways we could save money on your returns. But you hadn't really asked me about this. So I hadn't researched it."

What??

When I first read this story on Ed's blog post, I was irritated for him. And his wife and kids. He would never be able to recover the money he flushed down the toilet over decades.

He later said that it was worse than he had posted. He said he spent about $120,000 or so per year in taxes over much of the decade leading up to his revelation. But in the decade since, he hired a tax strategist and he paid exactly zero to Uncle Sam.

Zero!

> "Anyone may arrange his affairs so that his taxes shall be as low as possible; he is not bound to choose that pattern which best pays the treasury. There is not even a patriotic duty to increase one's taxes. Over and over again the Courts have said that there is nothing sinister in so arranging affairs as to keep taxes as low as possible. Everyone does it, rich and poor alike and all do right, for nobody owes any public duty to pay more than the law demands."
> – Judge Learned Hand, 2nd District Court of Appeals - 1934

Again, that wouldn't apply to everyone, but even if you could save half that much, wouldn't you want to know how? To be clear, I know Ed. He is a high-integrity guy, and he files honest returns. He is conservative by nature. That's how tax-beneficial this asset class can be!

Hopefully your CPA is better than that one. But I encourage you to be sure he or she is highly ethical, and at the same time looking for every possible tax advantage for you.

I hired the same tax strategist/CPA that saves Ed over $100k annually. He has saved me a boatload of taxes as well. If you want his contact info, email me at: paul@wellingscapital.com.

One more note: If you invest with a great Sponsor, they will solve many of these tax issues for you. They should know about these issues and manage most of them on your behalf.

Return of Capital

One of the issues your Sponsor will decide is how to treat cash distributions as they are disbursed. It is possible that your cash returns may be treated as a "return of capital" rather than taxable returns on investment. Depending on the structure of the investment, all of your distributions up to the full amount of your investment could be treated this way, and perhaps be non-taxable as a result. This will affect your basis in the asset, and may result in higher taxes later. Ask your CPA and Sponsor for details about what would be best for your situation.

Accelerated Depreciation through Cost Segregation

Depreciation is a method for allocating the cost of a tangible asset over its useful life. Since the IRS would not allow a million dollar tax deduction in the year of that million-dollar purchase, the million dollars is allocated via formula over the projected useful life of that asset. This provides a deduction to the income for the owner in each year the asset is depreciated.

For example, if a machine is purchased for a million dollars, and its useful life is 10 years, it would (typically – if straight line) be depreciated at $100,000 annually. If a million dollar building that houses that machine will be usable for decades, it might be depreciated over 39 years (typical IRS categories for permanent structures include 27.5 years and 39 years – but there are others). Land is not depreciable since its

---

If you're having trouble sleeping, you can check out the IRS depreciation code for yourself: www.irs.gov/publications/p946/ch04.html#en_US_2013_publink1000107554

---

value does not typically drop with use over time.

As a direct, fractional owner of commercial real estate, you get a direct benefit from the financial depreciation of the asset. This means your income will be reduced by the amount of the asset's depreciation that year. It is very likely, after making a new investment in a commercial multifamily property, that you will have many years where you get a healthy quarterly dividend check, but your annual K-1 shows a loss. (This is completely legit and above board of course.)

Your CPA undoubtedly knows this. You probably yawned as you skimmed through it. But you may not have been aware, and some accountants may not bother to tell you, that there is a way to dramatically accelerate your income deductions and tax savings using componentized depreciation, aka cost segregation.

The IRS code for Cost Segregation may actually be slightly more interesting than the last link on basic depreciation: www.irs.gov/ businesses/cost-segregation-audit-techniques-guide-chapter-2-legal-framework

---

Here's how it works in summary. A commercial real estate asset usually has components that wear out faster and need to be replaced more frequently than the structure as a whole. These components can be more quickly depreciated than the building itself.

For example, an apartment building may have a 27.5-year life for depreciation purposes. But many elements in and around the apartment may have a much shorter life and can be depreciated much sooner. These may include kitchen cabinets, appliances, plumbing fixtures, shelving and carpet. All of these can probably be depreciated on a 5-year schedule. Other items like paving and landscaping are considered improvements to the land, and can probably be written off over 15 years. And when you trash out a property for rehab, any deductions not yet taken can probably be fully depreciated at that time.

This may not sound like a big deal, but trust me, it can be an enormous tax savings over many years. My friend, Ted, used to provide cost segregation services to commercial property owners for a living. He showed me some of the numbers and I'll tell you that they were quite impressive. I recall that I wished I owned a commercial building so I could enjoy some of these benefits, but at the time I had an uninformed bias against commercial real estate, as I mentioned before. If you'd like to see an example of accelerated depreciation in action, go to our website: www.wellingscapital.com/accelerate-my-depreciation.

Correctly Classify Fully Deductible Repairs

It is easy for an uninformed clerk to classify all property rehab expenses as capital expenditures (Cap-Ex). Cap-Ex expenditures are depreciated over many years, as discussed above. Repairs to the property, however, are generally classified as expenses in the current year. These expenses do not have to be spread out over years.

A professional commercial multifamily accountant knows how to use the tax code to be sure every possible repair is deductible in the current period. A great asset manager will know the right questions to ask to be sure this is being maximized on behalf of his investors.

Refinance Tax-Free

Ever refinanced your home? Were you able to pull equity out of it to use for something you wanted? How much tax did you pay?

If your apartment complex has grown in value, as it should if operated well in a stable economic environment, you don't have to wait until you sell the property to safely extract some of the accumulated equity. Refinancing your commercial multifamily investment can be a great way to put cash in your pocket with no tax consequence.

Debt Service Coverage Ratio (DSCR) aka Debt Coverage Ratio (DCR): The ratio of cash available to the mortgage payment. This is a measure of the safety of the debt. Lenders typically want to see a minimum ratio of 1.2x (120%), but I like our projects to be at least 1.4x in the worst year.

If your Sponsor is considering this option, he will have a lender underwriting the deal, so he will likely not extract so much equity that it leaves the property short on operating capital or underwater in the event of a downturn. Nevertheless, you should ask your Sponsor how the refinance affects the Debt Service Coverage Ratio (DSCR) and how many months of principal and interest will be held in reserve to cover contingencies (we like to hold six months or more).

Here's an example of how this could work. Note that I am being overly simplistic for the sake of space. In the real world, I'd be calculating closing costs, capital improvements, and many other items.

Imagine you bought a 200-unit multifamily asset for $50,000 per unit – a total of $10 million with a seven-year loan of $7,500,000 (75% LTV – loan-to-value ratio). The loan was interest-only for the first few years.

The 7th year is upon you, and the cap rate is stable. Between your upgrades and strong multifamily demographics nationally, your Net Operating Income has gone up by 35%. The value of your property, which is the NOI divided by the cap rate (assume the same as when it was purchased), has therefore gone up 35% as well, to $13,500,000.

During the seven years, you have paid down the mortgage balance 12.6%, from $7,500,000 to about $6,555,000. The owners' equity was $2,500,000 at purchase. It has now grown to $6,945,000 ($13,500,000 value less $6,555,000 loan payoff).

> **Loan to Value Ratio (LTV).** This is a risk assessment metric used by lenders when determining a loan amount. Typically, lenders will lend up to about 70% to 80% of the purchase price of an asset. A higher loan amount results in a lower amount of cash (equity) needed for closing. This typically results in a higher return on investment since the profit (a bit lower with higher interest) is spread across a lower amount of investment. (This ROI improvement would not necessarily be the case in a season of very high interest rates because the high debt service reduces returns.)

Assuming you don't want to sell the property, you can refinance at 75% LTV again. 75% of $13.5 million is $10,125,000.

How much equity can you extract? Assuming a holdback of $1 million for capital improvements and mortgage payment reserves, the operator can extract about $2,570,000 ($10,125,000 new mortgage less $6,555,000 payoff old mortgage less $1 million holdback). This cash is returned to all of the investors, or can be invested in a new project. Because it is refinancing of a debt, there is no tax on this distribution.

Summary of tax breaks so far...

So continuing with this example... You've invested with a reputable Sponsor who has put together a single-use LLC to purchase an apartment complex for $10 million. You confirmed the structure of the deal with your tax strategist, who liked the direct investment opportunity. You did your own analysis of the asset by reviewing the MSA and the submarket. Your Sponsor hired a great property manager, and spent three years upgrading the interiors which drove significant rent increases and improved occupancy. Costs have been held in check, and the property has thrown off a healthy average 7% annual cash-on-cash return for the past seven years. You've already received almost 50% of your original investment as a result.

So how much have you paid in taxes?

The Sponsor is depreciating the appropriate percentage of the cost of the building and other improvements each year. Additionally, a cost segregation study allowed accountants to deduct dramatically more from the Net Operating Income of the property. Which is your NOI since you're a direct owner of this property. So far, for seven years, you've received a passive loss on your tax return each year. Yet you've pocketed almost half of what you originally invested.

Now you get word that the Sponsor is refinancing the property, and you will receive about 30% to 50% of what you originally invested in one day. Also tax-free, since it was generated through refinancing a debt. You've still paid exactly zero in taxes.

Wait, this sounds too good to be true. We'll have to pay the piper someday, right?

Yep. That *someday* is the day the property is sold. *Or is it?*

Defer Taxes at Sale Through a 1031 Exchange

You may be familiar with the 1031 Exchange. This is an IRS-sanctioned vehicle that allows you to effectively exchange one asset for another of "like kind." Capital gain taxes on the sale of the asset you are selling are not cancelled or avoided, but rather deferred until the sale of the second (or future non-exchanged) property at a later date. At the time of the "final" (non-exchanged) sale, all of the accrued gain for previously exchanged properties will be paid at once.

> You can learn more about selling your asset using a 1031 Starker Exchange here: www.irs.gov/uac/Like-Kind-Exchanges-Under-IRC-Code-Section-1031
> I must say that this is one of the clearest explanations of the 1031 I have read. Enjoy!

While it may sound better to you to pay it as you go, remember our taxed versus tax-free penny doubled daily example. It's virtually always much better to avoid taxes for as long as you can. It's easily provable and well documented.

So what is this "like-kind" provision? Does that mean a 300-unit Dallas apartment complex must be traded for another 300-unit complex in Fort Worth? Not at all. The IRS regulations for real estate exchanges are actually very broad. The website I cited in the information box is very helpful here...

> Both the relinquished property you sell and the replacement property you buy must meet certain requirements.
>
> Both properties must be held for use in a trade or business or for investment. Property used primarily for personal use, like a primary residence or a second home or vacation home, does not qualify for like-kind exchange treatment.
>
> Both properties must be similar enough to qualify as "like-kind." Like-kind property is property of the same nature, character or class. Quality or grade does not matter. Most real estate will be like-kind to other real estate. For example, real property that is improved with a residential rental house is like-kind to vacant land. One exception for real estate is that property within the United States is not like-kind to property outside of the United States. Also, improvements that are conveyed without land are not of like kind to land.
>
> Real property and personal property can both qualify as exchange properties under Section 1031; but real property can never be like-kind to personal property. In personal property exchanges, the rules pertaining to what qualifies as like-kind are more restrictive than the rules pertaining to real property. As an example, cars are not like-kind to trucks.

The law was derived from the possibility that properties could be swapped, and there would be no cash to pay taxes on the gain. But it was broadened to allow the sale of one property and the purchase of another within about six months, with the funds from the sale of the first property held by an intermediary. Again, from the IRS site...

So what does this mean to you as a multifamily investor? It could mean that you are able to sell ("exchange") your property and... after paying minimal taxes on your returns over a number of years... after paying no taxes on proceeds from a refinance... that you are able to defer the capital gains tax as well.

In July of 2013, Jason Mak purchased an 81-unit apartment building in Riverside, CA. Paying $3.1 million dollars for the property, he immediately set out to improve the building. He worked on the business side, evicting bad tenants and improving management efficiencies, as well as on the physical condition of the property, adding a new roof and elevator, painting, landscaping, and more. After increasing occupancy from 60% to 95% and stabilizing the entire operation, Jason sold the property for $5.5 million dollars in the spring of 2015. Overall, he netted a final profit of $2,000,000 on the two-year apartment turnaround!

Had Jason simply sold this deal, he would have needed to pay close to $600,000 in capital gains tax, but he knew better. Jason used a 1031 exchange to parlay his cash into two new properties, a 24-unit apartment building and an upscale office building. Although reducing the number of units, Jason was able to buy nicer properties in significantly better locations that will be easier to manage and increase his ability to grow wealth *(https://www.biggerpockets.com/renewsblog/2015/09/24/1031-exchanges-real-estate/ Accessed July 17, 2016).*

What are the time limits to complete a Section 1031 Deferred Like-Kind Exchange?

While a like-kind exchange does not have to be a simultaneous swap of properties, you must meet two time limits or the entire gain will be taxable. These limits cannot be extended for any circumstance or hardship except in the case of presidentially declared disasters.

The first limit is that you have 45 days from the date you sell the relinquished property to identify potential replacement properties. The identification must be in writing, signed by you and delivered to a person involved in the exchange like the seller of the replacement property or the qualified intermediary. However, notice to your attorney, real estate agent, accountant or similar persons acting as your agent is not sufficient.

Replacement properties must be clearly described in the written identification. In the case of real estate, this means a legal description, street address or distinguishable name. Follow the IRS guidelines for the maximum number and value of properties that can be identified.

The second limit is that the replacement property must be received and the exchange completed no later than 180 days after the sale of the exchanged property or the due date (with extensions) of the income tax return for the tax year in which the relinquished property was sold, whichever is earlier. The replacement property received must be substantially the same as property identified within the 45-day limit described above.

Die and pay taxes?

Is it possible to completely avoid capital gains tax, too?

If you have enjoyed the tax benefits of depreciating your property for a number of years... then performed a 1031 exchange at the time of sale... then perhaps another... you will likely be faced with a very small tax basis... and a very large taxable gain. Which is usually still better than paying taxes along the way.

If your estate is set up properly, however, it may be possible for your heirs to reset the basis of the assets at the time of their inheritance. This is referred to as a step-up in basis. Their assets *could* reflect the enormous growth possible from tax deferrals, and they could start with a clean slate: The opportunity to start depreciating these assets again from the beginning. This can often be more tax-efficient than gifting the property to heirs prior to death.

For example, suppose you find a trustworthy Sponsor and invest $2 million in multifamily assets. The property basis depreciates down to $1 million over a number of years. In addition to whatever income you received, the property has appreciated to a value of $4 million. Before your passing, one option is to sell your share in the property, and pay a hefty $450,000 capital gains tax on the $3 million gain, leaving heirs with a $3,550,000 net inheritance. If it could be arranged to pass your direct investment in the assets to your heirs, however, they may be able to step-up their basis in the asset to the value at the time of inheritance of $4 million. If they choose to sell the asset at that time, their gain would be zero and their net asset value around $4 million.

Note that there may be a cap on the step-up in basis. Ask your CPA or tax strategist for more details.

Do you see why I refer to commercial multifamily investing as the most powerful vehicle to create multi-generational wealth?

Self-Directed Retirement Fund Options

Another tax savings measure is to directly invest in multifamily properties through a self-directed IRA. I have had a self-directed SEP IRA and a self-directed Roth IRA for well over a decade, and I only regret not doing this sooner. If you have a 401(k), SEP, or another tax-sheltering retirement plan on your own or through your employer, you can usually roll this into a self-directed IRA.

Self-directed IRAs can take the form of a Roth IRA, a SEP IRA or a Solo 401(k). The Roth IRA allows after-tax contributions, but gains are never taxed. SEP and Solo 401(k) plans allow pre-tax contributions, but they grow tax-free, and withdrawals are taxed (theoretically at a lower rate in the future).

While a traditional retirement plan had a small, fixed number of investment options, a self-directed IRA opens up a significant number of investment options. Though there are limitations on the type of investment and the way it is handled, the flexibility of this vehicle is almost "dangerous."

The Self-Directed retirement account is not for everyone...

➤ If you're a fan of the Social Security system, and you like the ROI you're getting on the 7.65% FICA (really 15.3%) investment you make from each paycheck, then the self-directed IRA is probably not for you. The IRA puts you in control of your own destiny.

➤ If you love to invest in the latest investment scheme or crazy invention your neighbor is working on in his basement, the self-directed IRA could get you in trouble. But at least you have the freedom to lose your money as you see fit.

➤ If you think your plan administrator can do a better job picking investment options (typically mutual funds or bond funds) for you, then you don't need the flexibility offered by the self-directed product. There are easier and cheaper ways to accomplish your investment goals. (Honestly, many people would be *far better* off with this option. Especially those in the second category above.)

But if you have come to a place where you have the knowledge and desire to safely invest in multifamily commercial real estate, and you want to use your retirement account to do it, then a self-directed retirement plan is the only option I am aware of.

I have used my self-directed SEP IRA and Roth IRA for a variety of real estate transactions over the years. One Spring, a friend approached me about buying his friend's home. He had fallen on hard times, was way behind on his mortgage, and just wanted out. He said he would sell it for a few thousand above the payoff. This would allow him to avoid foreclosure and give him enough to start a new life in Kentucky. He needed to make it happen in a few days.

I contracted to purchase the home for $125,000 through my Roth IRA. After closing, I spent a month or two arranging for contractors to spruce it up with new carpet, paint, appliances and landscaping. All funded through the Roth IRA.

After selling it for $172,000 that Fall, I was able to put my costs plus almost a $20,000 profit back into the IRA. All tax free at the time, and tax free permanently. Because it was a Roth IRA, it meant the original funds I had contributed were after-tax. So all gains to the IRA would have no tax. Not then… not ever. Much better than the short-term capital gain I would have had to pay.

There are many great administrators available, and they will handle the paperwork on every transaction for you to be sure you remain in compliance. They will also handle your annual returns and help you with income from the vehicle when it's time to receive it. I use a full-service firm that provides a diverse menu of services and options, but they are more costly than some discount services that allow you to do most of the work on your own. For my current self-directed IRA administrator recommendation, please visit: www.wellingscapital.com/IRA.

Avoid Passive Loss Limitations

As we have discussed, commercial real estate provides unique opportunities to earn a significant passive income while simultaneously receiving losses on your tax return. These losses are limited to $25,000 per year in some cases (they may be carried forward though), and may be limited further by your income if you're an active investor. Passive investors are able to bank and carry forward passive losses with no limit on time or amount.

If you spend most of your professional time in the world of real estate, and if you work more than 750 hours per year, there may be a way for you to deduct much more by qualifying as a *Real Estate Professional* according to IRS guidelines. There are so many qualifiers to this process that I don't want to develop this idea any further here. I just wanted you to know it is possible. Talk to your CPA or tax strategist to learn more.

As the old saying goes, there are two things you can't avoid in this world: death and taxes. Some people dread the latter more than the former. Commercial real estate investing provides a wonderful opportunity to largely avoid this unpleasant aspect of life in this fallen world.

Chapter 10 – Finding A Deal Partner
Part I: Integrity and Ethics

So hopefully I've effectively convinced you that commercial multifamily investing is one of the safest, surest paths to create multi-generational wealth. *The Perfect Investment.* If I've done my job well, I'm hopeful that you're considering one of these options:

(A) You want to jump in and start your own multifamily investment firm.

-- OR--

(B) You want to find a trustworthy investment firm/Sponsor to invest with.

If you're considering option A, you may want to skim this section so you'll have an idea what type of firm you need to create to attract investors. I would also strongly recommend you review www.multifamilypartner.com. They are a phenomenal resource for new active apartment investors. This is a program from my friends at Multifamily Partner Program, who I've mentioned elsewhere in this book. If you're considering option B, you'll want to utilize these criteria to help determine who you'll trust with your hard-earned funds.

Before I launch into the factors that you should consider in an investment partner, I want to try to explode one myth about decision-making. Uncovering this can give you the ability to make better decisions in almost any area of life.

The Myth of Objectivity

No one is completely objective. Sales trainees are taught that buyers buy whatever they want to buy, based on their right-brain desires. Then they use their left-brain to come up with objective reasons to justify their decision. (The reasons they give their spouse.) If you think through your last large purchase or investment, you'll probably conclude that this is what you did, too.

I offended one of the last people I explained this to. He claimed he was totally objective. Then he went on to explain his decision process, which only proved my point. (I didn't drive the point home any further. He did a fine job on his own.)

We all make countless numbers of decisions this way every year. I recently spent hundreds for a pair of Cole Haan wingtip shoes. When my wife commented on this, I gave her a list of left-brain reasons. "They'll last well over a decade, so the cost per year is less than the cost of your steak last night." "They're made of fine Italian leather, so they breathe better." "They're more comfortable, so I'll have more energy when I travel." Funny, I never thought of these things before I hit put them in my Amazon shopping cart. I just really wanted them.

I don't mean to be offensive, but if you used the gas mileage reason to justify your motorcycle purchase, or the safety argument to buy your Hummer, you may have done the same thing. Not that these reasons are untrue. But let's face it. We usually follow our innate desires when making a purchase, then we explain the decision to others using objective reasoning.

Since everyone makes decisions this way, to varying degrees, why do I even bring this up? And what is the remedy? I think that just acknowledging this will go a long way toward dealing with the pitfalls inherent in decision-making.

If you know you're likely to make decisions based primarily on desire, and secondarily on reason, you are better positioned to be as objective as possible. You will be able to filter the factors below through a better understanding of who you are, and if you're wise, you'll get someone else involved. Run your big decisions by a spouse, friend or professional who has virtually nothing to lose or gain by your decision. I've learned to do this, and it has helped me avoid potentially costly errors in many areas of my life.

Racking the Shotgun and Looking for Flies

Invest with high integrity people. You'd think this would go without saying, but it needs to be reviewed. In fact, I cannot think of a more important category where the *Objectivity Myth* can cloud your thinking.

When you're making an investment through a Sponsor/ investment partner, you are first and foremost buying that person and their team. A knowledgeable, high integrity person can often rescue a marginal deal, and a low integrity person can mess up any great deal.

Do not be sucked into believing something that looks too good to be true. Because invariably, it is. There are rare exceptions, but I can't recall many.

Marketing guru Perry Marshall tells the story of his friend, John, who went to Vegas to learn to be a card shark after dropping out of high school. His desire was to assure that Sin City lived up to its reputation as "Lost Wages" for many of the 50,000 visitors who showed up there daily.

He quickly realized he needed a mentor, so he joined up with Rob, who agreed to train him for a share of the profits. His mentor taught him how to find "marks." Suckers. People he could cheat out of their cash.

The veteran took John into a bar and quietly slipped a sawed off shotgun out of his jacket. He slipped it under the table and pressed the lever as if to load it. Instead of inserting a shell, he loudly snapped it back shut with that sharp, signature sound shotguns are known for. What enthusiasts call "racking the shotgun."

A few heads in the crowd snapped around to see where the sound came from. Everyone else was oblivious, absorbed in the haze of Vegas revelry.

He turned to his trainee and said, "John, everyone who turned around is NOT a mark. Don't play poker with them." He smiled and continued: "Your job is to play poker with everyone else."

My friend, there are people out there who are looking for marks. They know how to discover the gullible investors who they can take advantage of. It makes me sick to think that some people think it's acceptable to take advantage of other people, and steal from them through the channel of real estate investing.

I wrote this book, in part, to be sure that you would not be one of their Marks.

I have to admit...I was a victim myself. I mentioned this earlier. My business partner and I sold our staffing company to a publicly traded firm in the 90s. I suddenly had years of income in my bank account, and I had to figure out where to invest it. A friend introduced me to a guy in Charlotte who had developed an amazing platform to trade international currencies, or so he said. He was making a 2 to 3% *monthly* return, and he split it with his investors. A sure thing. I talked to others who were making money, then invested $100,000.

Fast forward two years. After declaring zero income on his tax return and $900,000 on his mortgage application, the IRS matched the two and put him on trial. Amazingly, when given the chance to reduce his 150-year sentence in exchange for the millions he stole from 2,000-plus investors, hidden in offshore bank accounts, he chose the longer jail sentence.

The FBI eventually returned 16% of investors' money. This was a hard lesson for me... and a few thousand others.

Honestly, though it was painful, this was one brick in the wall of my decision to pursue multifamily investing.

If you've had a similar experience, say it aloud with me now:

"I refuse to be taken in by any more too-good-to-be-true schemes. I will invest in proven assets with reasonable returns through high integrity asset managers with proven track records. Amen."

(Ok, well you don't have to say amen. But I do pray that you won't fall prey to these types of greedy schemers.)

Looking for flies...

One time I was meeting with the owner of a small oil company west of Austin. He invested with asset managers in the oilfields, and he had some great advice on how to sniff out unscrupulous operators. In his best Texas drawl, he said, "Whenever anyone is asking me for money, I start lookin' for flies." He paused.

"Flies?" I asked.

"Yep, flies. Whenever I see a fly buzzing up above... no matter how good the deal looks... I know there's some horse manure (he used a different word) down beneath. I politely show him the door."

That was it, in simple Texan. If he picked up the tiniest insincerity or lack of integrity, even if all the numbers and plans looked foolproof, he walked. Through past mistakes, he had made a decision in advance – using his left-brain – to override his right-brain desire for profit if the tiniest thing seemed amiss.

Like all of us, his fear of loss was greater than his desire for gain. But unlike many of us, he had been burned enough times to learn when to walk away.

If I could have heard and applied that advice I would have saved myself countless heartaches and losses. From Tommy Chamberlain's 2nd grade baseball card trade ("I'll give you all the baseball cards in this shoebox for just one card – your Pete Rose") to my high school sweetheart who cheated on me ("My boss scheduled me and I was at work all evening") to the five-year old Honda Odyssey I bought on eBay with (supposedly) only 16,000 miles ("An older couple from New Jersey had it and they always took the train").

I'm happy to say I have learned to look for flies. I recently did a U-turn when I saw the exact car I was looking for at a used car lot in a nearby city. This late model Mercedes E 350 had the exact colors, features, low mileage and reasonable price I had been holding out for. It even had the little spoiler on the trunk as a bonus.

After taking it for a quick spin, I looked at my watch and realized that I was going to be late if I stood around to haggle with the dealer, a stylin' young guy with a nice looking gold watch. "I've got to run. I told my wife I'd be home by six."

"Tell her you got stuck in traffic," he said.

That answered all my questions about the car. As I drove away, I began to rationalize that he was just a dealer. It could have been the best car ever. Garaged, faithfully maintained, and only driven below the speed limit with nearly all highway miles. And after all, it was black with a tan leather interior.

But then I heard that Texan's voice and I swatted the fly away with a smile. That was three months ago, and I'm still holding out for the perfect car at the right price. I've passed his dealership many times, but I've never been tempted to stop again.

Intuition. Gut feeling. Sixth sense. Following your heart.

I don't know how this all works. But quantum physics is giving us hints about how our brains were designed with abilities to read people and situations in ways that seem supernatural. Rather than prattle on about this point any further right here, I will reserve more thoughts in this vein for anyone who wants to visit: www.wellingscapital.com/supernatural-investing.

So what does this have to do with multifamily investing?

Everything.

I think I've made my point, but please, *please* don't invest your hard earned money with anyone who does not pass the buzzing fly test. Don't be the clueless *mark* for an unscrupulous operator. Look in their eyes and ask them hard questions. Fly across the country if you need to. Or make them come to you.

Questions...

Speaking of hard questions, what should you ask to check out their integrity? What should you do? I think you can figure that out for the most part, but I will throw in a few thoughts that may help.

I'd start with a detailed Google search to see what you can learn about all of the parties involved. Search out everything they were part of or owned in the past. You can learn a lot on LinkedIn, Facebook and from a copy of their resume. Check some un-offered references. You may be able to stop right there if you see a fly abuzz.

➤ Ask them if they've ever declared bankruptcy. Why?
➤ Ask about any felony charges or convictions.
➤ Any SEC or state security commission violations?
➤ Do they have any issues with State Attorney Generals?

This is a big deal in this business. There are a lot of rules about who and what and how you can raise investment dollars for real estate syndications, limited partnerships and other investment opportunities where the Sponsor/syndicator relies on pooling the funds of a group of individual investors.

Many of the rules changed recently, and some interpretations may evolve further. You can get information and links on the latest regulations on our website at: www.wellingscapital.com/SEC.

As part of your integrity screening process, I recommend you Google the various names of the company and individuals to see what you may find out.

One time I was checking out a small Dallas company that syndicated in the oil and gas business. The guy bragged about his stellar track record, but Google told a different story. It turns out he had a number of negative online reviews, and several states had charged him with violations due to his syndication practices. Pennsylvania had barred him from ever soliciting its citizens to invest. My IRA administrator, who apparently found more information, told me they strongly recommended that their clients not invest there.

That's a horsefly buzzing around, and armed with this information, I ran in the other direction.

There are a number of SEC regulations that unscrupulous or marginally unethical operators openly break or don't take that seriously. With a minimal amount of knowledge about these regulations, you can screen your prospective Sponsor to check their knowledge and ethics.

There are many more questions you can ask.

➤ Tell me about your history in business?

➤ What is your background in this business?

➤ Why did you get into this business?

➤ What would you do in the event that…?

Summary of SEC Regulations for Real Estate Syndications*

- When a company raises money for real estate, it is technically deemed a security.
- The company that is raising money can raise an unlimited amount of money without registering a public sale through the SEC (depends on type of security).
- Even if the transaction only involves a few investors, the company or entrepreneur wanting to raise capital still needs to provide the proper framework and disclosure documentation; however, these requirements are significantly less than what is required for a public offering.
- The company must generally sell the securities to "accredited investors" and may also include up to 35 "non-accredited" investors as long as they are sophisticated.
- Under the law, Sponsors (aka syndicators) will be required to take "reasonable steps" to verify that the purchasers are, in fact, accredited investors.
- Securities offerings can utilize general advertising as long as the offering company takes additional steps to verify investors' accredited status before consummating any sale (depending on offering type).
- The securities that are sold are "restricted" so they cannot be resold during the first year.

* **Important Note**: This is a general overview and does not apply to every specific offering, security type or investment. Consult the SEC and your counsel to see how these rules may apply in your situation. *And did I mention that I'm not an attorney?*

On the subject of character, there are a number of other less obvious things to look for...

➤ How do they treat the waiter, the flight attendant or the taxi driver? Do they remember their names? Tip them well? Or treat them like 2nd class servants?

➤ How do they treat their employees and other staff?

➤ How do they talk about people, companies or partners

they've had conflict with?

➤ How do they speak of their spouse and children?

➤ How do they view tenants and former tenants?

➤ How do they speak about property managers, vendors, attorneys and others who are involved in their business?

It goes without saying that the way they view and treat others says a lot about their character and ultimately their ability to successfully invest and manage your money.

I've spent a lot of time on the issues of ethics and character, but I don't believe I've overstated my point. Now let's move on to the other issues that can help you determine a Sponsor/investor fit.

Chapter 11 – Finding a Deal Partner Part II: Strategy and Team

By reading this volume, hopefully you have enough information to do a few important things:

1. Understand your desired investment goals and strategy enough to evaluate a Sponsor.

2. Understand the terminology and basics of the business well enough to ask your prospective Sponsor intelligent questions.

What's Your Strategy?

Using what you've already learned, you can make inquiries into your potential deal partner's fit in the areas that are most important to you. Review their website and other marketing materials to see if they share your values. Do their strategy and tactics match your goals? Can you review their business plan? Can you talk to previous investors?

Have you bought into my proposal that the value-add strategy provides superior returns, safety and stability amongst the options in this asset class? If so, does your prospective partner share this belief? Do their plans for adding value make logical and financial sense?

Perhaps you want to follow another strategy. There are other great ways to make money in multifamily. Here are a few...

New development carries higher risk and *potentially* higher returns (or potential losses). Land acquisition, rezoning, local approvals, construction bidding and management, marketing, leasing up the property, market timing, financing and refinancing and a hundred other issues may result in *great* rewards… or not. The still-empty streets of partially developed subdivisions from the Great Recession are a reminder to all of us that the development strategy carries great risk, even for experienced developers.

Buying **stabilized, previously improved Class B properties** with optimized rents allow you to enjoy a prior owner's value-adds. The cost is high, but the heavy lifting has been done. Or you may want to purchase a **Class A property** (either a newly developed property or one that was built in the past decade, for example). Some refer to these as *momentum-plays*.

Or perhaps you want to roll the dice with an ***unstabilized* property**. A lower entrance price, a whole lot of work, and no guarantee of success. A potential homerun if you succeed. Possible ruin if you lose.

Maybe you'd rather drop down to ***Class C or even Class D***. Higher crime, lower rent, higher turnover, and more difficult tenants. Or other factors that limit your upside growth. An opportunity to maintain the property without the efforts to add value. (Value-add strategy doesn't work as well since the area usually won't support much higher rents from upgrades.) Lower purchase price and lower resale later. Likely higher cash on cash returns reward investors along the way, but profit payoff at the end typically not as significant. Make sure to ask your pre-screened property management firm how they feel about placing their staff in that location.

Whatever your strategy, you will want to investigate and interview your prospective Sponsor to see if their strategy and plans match your goals. In the following pages, I will lay out some of the critical items you should be asking them about.

1. Team. Tell me about your team. Ask them for info on the major team members they should have onboard before ever discussing a deal. Talk to a few of those folks about this Sponsor. You may wish to ask them detailed questions as well.

So who are some of the key team members?

A. **Property Management Firm.** As we discussed before, along with location, the right property manager will likely account for about 2/3rds of the success of this investment.

B. **Broker.** Most multifamily buyers work with multiple brokers on the ground in a market. It's critical that the Sponsor develop a reputation of trust with the Broker by staying in touch, following through on commitments, and not re-trading during the process of finalizing deals.

C. **Entity Attorney.** Your operator will probably set up sole-purpose entities for any asset they acquire. A solid attorney will guide them in this process, and assure that the entity is in a position to pass along depreciation and shield its investors from liability.

D. **SEC Attorney.** If your owner/operator is syndicating this investment (raising the equity through a variety of investors), they will need a private, real estate focused SEC attorney. It is important to get this right since this team member will make sure that all of the documents are in compliance with federal and state regulations and that all documents are filed correctly.

An acquaintance of mine was putting together a group of investors to buy mineral rights. This grew from a handful of friends to their friends and others he really didn't know. The state Attorney General reviewed their paperwork and determined that he did not comply with appropriate regulations. Though the investments had a nice return, and no investors had complained, the Attorney General ordered him to shut down the fund and give all of the investors their money back. This story has a happy ending because all the investors loved the investment, and the guy re-filed the paperwork. Correctly this time. (It cost him a lot – especially with regulators breathing down his neck.) All the investors reinvested and they are still enjoying nice returns today.

E. **Bank.** This type of operation requires several accounts (escrow accounts, capital reserves, mortgage reserves, operational accounts, etc.). The strength of the bank and the relationships with their management are more important than the fees.

F. **CPA/Tax Strategist.** As an investor or a Sponsor, you want to do everything by the book, and make sure you are maximizing your legal tax savings.

G. **Corporate Insurer.** There are several insurance policies involved with this business. These include commercial fire/hazard/owner liability, commercial liability, and personal umbrella insurance.

A great insurance broker can save you thousands, and it's worth having them shop your policies at least annually.

Your Sponsor should also shop other brokers. My multifamily business partner owns a commercial strip center and he was paying $5,700 for insurance annually when his bank offered to give him a quote. They came in at $6,300, so he was feeling pretty good about his original deal. He asked a new broker to try for a better rate. After lots of shopping, he surprised Brian with a policy from a different carrier for only $2,875. It was tempting to be irritated that he didn't get a better rate earlier, but he was happy to have the savings going forward.

H. Title/Closing Attorney. Your Sponsor will want to utilize a closing firm that specializes in commercial real estate, specifically multifamily.

You may be wondering why I went through this list of key team members. As you interview Sponsors who will be handling hundreds of thousands of your hard-earned funds, you will want to be sure that they know what they're doing and that they have their act together. Asking them about their team will give you insight into this. And it may show them you know what you're talking about, which certainly can't hurt if you get into negotiations with them about terms.

2. Asset Management. The Asset Manager is typically the Sponsor, or syndicator. As the Asset Manager, he will be responsible for everything about the investment and the property from purchase through refinance through final sale.

You will want to learn as much as possible about the asset manager and his team. How will he choose and hold the Property Manager accountable? How often and how deeply will he be involved in overseeing the property? What will his role be in executing a value-add or other revenue enhancement strategy? How much experience does he have in marketing, and how will he assist the Property Manager in this arena?

If you are going to talk with the Asset Manager, I would really focus on understanding his value-add strategy. Ask why he thinks he can increase rents that much. Do the comparable properties in the submarket really support these increases? Ask him to see a list of the comparable properties to support his plan. Check them out yourself.

Re-trading is when the buyer takes the list of items found in the property's physical inspection and seeks to re-negotiate the price to compensate. This can cause a very difficult situation for the seller on a number of levels, and the seller and broker want to avoid it to the extent they can do so. Everything could be up for grabs, and a shortsighted buyer can cause a very awkward situation for the seller. I say "shortsighted" because a buyer who does this will not likely get the opportunity to do it again... at least not with that broker and those he is in contact with.

Think about the problems that re-trading could cause the seller...

1. If the buyer is hard-nosed and wants to push this, it could result in a much lower sales price.
2. It puts the broker in an awkward position, and both the seller and buyer may ask him to take a commission cut ("You're the expert after all. How did this happen?").
3. It could cause the deal to fall apart. This could be devastating for the seller and broker since they would have to take the asset back to the market and start over. This obviously causes a delay, but now the property has a "mark" on it. The initial group of buyers has likely moved on (this is almost two months after the Call for Offers), and everyone will wonder what's wrong with the property. It will be eyed with suspicion and may sell for even less now. To complicate this further, a seller has often timed the sale for the due date of their loan. This delay could cause serious problems for the seller.

The buyer knows all this, which puts him at a negotiating advantage. In the big picture, however, a buyer who pulls these stunts is condemning his own future in that market. What broker would work with a buyer who significantly renegotiates terms and puts deals at risk? This is why brokers carefully screen buyers, and may not recommend the highest bidder.

Ask the Asset Manager about the critical amenities that renters are asking for in this submarket. While a beautiful clubhouse and office are impressive, the latest surveys show renters' top priority is fast and reliable Internet service. For an up-to-date survey of the highest priority renter amenities, go to: www.wellingscapital.com/amenities.

3. Investor Relations. As an investor, it will be nice to know how much contact you will have with the asset management team initially and over time. Will they invite you to tour the property before you make a decision? What about checking up on the property a year or two later?

What type of reports will you receive? How often? Can you review a sample report? Are their reports completely transparent, showing a full picture of investor returns as well as fees and distributions to the Sponsor?

What is the plan for distributions? How consistent? How much of the profit will be put back in the property for capital improvements and how will that affect my payouts?

What would generate a cash call (request for more cash) from investors? Have they ever had a cash call? Why?

4. Exit Strategy. There are many exit strategies, and each one has advantages and disadvantages. Your desire for regular cash flow versus long-term appreciation, as well as your need for tax savings will inform your strategy. Does your Sponsor's plan accommodate these goals? Does he have a definite plan?

In general, you should understand if your Sponsor plans to…

> ➤ Buy and hold long-term, with periodic refinance and a goal of paying off the debt.
> ➤ Systematically refinance or infuse equity to buy you out.
> ➤ Sell in a specific time period – with or without the option of a 1031 tax-deferred exchange into a new asset.
> ➤ Automatically return your proceeds, or give you the option to utilize your matured investment to "cascade-up" to more assets at the time of a liquidity event (refi-

nance or sale).

Commercial mortgages may have an amortization schedule similar to that of your home (say 20 or 30 years – often with a few years interest-only on the front end), but the term on the note is much shorter. A typical commercial mortgage comes due in five, seven or ten years. The property must be sold or refinanced at this time. Do you understand your Sponsor's plan for that event?

5. Private Placement Memorandum & Subscription Agreement. Be sure to actually read the PPM provided by the Sponsor. This is a long, legal document, but it's more than that. It describes the legal and operational relationship between you, as the investor, and the Sponsor. Any issue that was discussed along the way, and any question you have about the legal relationship, should be covered here.

For example, what do you do if you want to cash in your investment? How will it be valued? Can you sell it back to the Sponsor? Can you sell it on the open market? Will the Sponsor offer it to other investors? What will you be charged if you sell your position?

There are dozens of other questions, some you never thought of, that will be answered in this document, so examine it carefully.

6. Sponsor Compensation. How does the Sponsor get paid? And how will this affect your returns and long-term value? What do they have to lose if this goes south? Do they have skin in the game? Is their compensation tied to performance?

There are just too many possible structures to cover here, and I am afraid it would be unfair to many if I trumpet one. Every situation is different. Every Sponsor is different. Large equity partners may persuade a Sponsor to model returns in a way that is different from the Sponsor's norm. The class and

location of the asset may dictate a different structure as well.
There are some common fees that will be helpful for you
to know about, and I will list them at a high level here.

➤ **Fee.** This is a one-time fee paid to the Sponsor for
pulling the deal together. This compensates them for
some of the overhead and general/administrative costs
that they experience in the long process of researching
deals and putting together all the pieces. Investors are
willing to pay these fees to get access to the opportunity. These fees are rolled into the cost of the acquisition.

➤ **Asset Management Fee.** This is an ongoing fee paid
to the Sponsor for the management of the asset. (This
is different from the Property Manager's fee.) This
includes record-keeping, property inspections, ongoing
oversight of the property manager and construction
crews, accounting, tax returns, investor relations and
distributions, etc.

➤ **Carried Interest.** This goes by a variety of names. It
is the ownership earned by the Sponsor in exchange
for the successful management, profitable ongoing
returns, and long-term value increase of the asset. A
good Syndication deal will typically reward the investors first. After established hurdles are passed, the
Sponsor will earn an ownership stake. This type of
structure ensures that the Sponsor's interests are
aligned with investors since they are not activated until
investors reach certain return levels.

In certain models, where investors earn a high
preferred return first, any returns above that level
could be split with a percentage of the balance going to
the Sponsor.

➤ **Disposition Fee.** This is a one-time fee associated with the sale or refinance of the asset. This is a time when investors often reap the rewards of their patience. There is a tremendous amount of work for the Asset Manager in either of these actions and they are typically compensated for these efforts.

➤ **Loan Guarantor Fees.** Being approved for a large commercial loan requires experience and a significant personal balance sheet. Sometimes that means two different parties will be required to guarantee the loan. Sometimes a Sponsor is in a position to be the guarantor, but other times he is not. In that case, he will look to investors or a third party to sign the loan documents. Since these are often non-recourse loans, the risk to the signer is typically limited to fraud and the introduction of environmental hazards at the property. If you are in a position to sign the loan docs, *you may be able to collect a one-time fee.* This may be paid as a flat fee, or awarded as an ownership stake in the asset.

In addition to these fees, Sponsors may be compensated on a pari passu basis for any money they invest in the project. Pari passu is a Latin word meaning "on equal footing." Which means the Sponsor's cash investment will be on equal footing with other cash investors. Again, the goal is alignment of interests between the investors and the Sponsor.

Some Sponsors elect to leave a portion of their acquisition fees in the deal, and these funds are treated on a pari passu basis with other investors' funds. This can be advantageous to everyone because the Sponsor will have dollars being treated the same as other investors.

You may feel cynical and think that these funds were not in the Sponsor's account in the first place. But trust me... there is massive effort put into bringing every multifamily investment opportunity to the table. The opportunity to passively invest in these projects is a privilege for most investors, and this fee is well worth it. I have sat on both sides of this table, and I can tell you that the typical fees and returns are fair and equitable to both parties.

> When we work in a market, we try to develop relationships with all types of professionals who may be involved in the commercial property arena. In addition to brokers, this may include closing attorneys, lenders, property managers and the local apartment marketing magazines. We even got to know the local Cort Furniture Rental reps in a few markets. They often have an inside scoop on what is happening at the apartments where they rent for furnished corporate rentals.

There are other fees including brokerage at acquisition, brokerage at sale and property management that are sometimes collected by parties to the transaction, but I personally believe it is usually best for the Sponsor to compensate others for these efforts and stay focused on the many other important tasks involved in maximizing returns on the purchase, operation and sale of this asset. I am a licensed real estate broker, but I have no desire to collect brokerage fees from any multifamily deal I'm involved in (though I don't think this would be unethical in any way).

While you, as an investor, want to make as much as possible from this investment, you should also want your Sponsor to do well, too. It only makes sense to align the goals of the investors and the Sponsor as much as possible.

That's one thing I absolutely love about this business, in fact. When done right, there are no losers. Everyone wins. The Seller, the Brokers, the Lender, the Investors, the Sponsor, the Property Management team, the Tenants and their families, and the next Buyer.

Which brings me to my final point about partnering with the right deal Sponsor…

7. Quality of Life. About a year ago, I was speaking with an experienced multifamily investor about improving a community we planned to acquire. I mentioned that one of my major planned changes would not have an immediate and obvious impact on the bottom line. We couldn't raise rents and it wasn't an urgent health, safety or deferred maintenance issue. "We just need to do this because it's the right thing to do."

The investor vigorously disagreed. "No way! If it doesn't have a clear and measurable impact on the bottom line, it should never be done. Don't fall into that way of thinking. Only do things that directly increase rents and reduce vacancy."

While I agree that every expenditure needs to be carefully weighed for its effectiveness, I do not agree that every expense item will have a direct, measurable impact on the bottom line. We are creating communities here. A place where babies are born, children are raised, newlyweds celebrate and the elderly spend their final years on earth.

Some things just need to be done because they're right. Some fences need to be built. Others need to be torn down. Some walls just need to be painted over. Some pools need to be repaired and some barbeque pits need to be refurbished.

I could give you pages and pages of documentation for why doing the right thing is just smart. I could prove to you that creating the right multifamily environment will result in happier employees, a much happier and higher quality tenant community, lower employee and tenant turnover, more referrals… and ultimately higher profits and higher value.

But I'm not even arguing that point here. We are not just physical beings. There is a mystical, spiritual component to all of us. Whether we are Sponsors or investors, staff or tenants, elderly or millennial, we were all created to be part of something lovely and good and right. We all crave that intangible satisfaction that comes with beauty. We were made to love and be loved.

As human beings with influence over housing and employees, we are called to love our neighbors as ourselves. My tenants are my neighbors. As a Sponsor, asset manager and multifamily investor, one of the ways I love them is to make apartment complexes into communities. And turn units into homes.

From ApartmentLife.org:
"In a survey of apartment residents, half said they didn't have any friends within their community. Apartment *communities* are full of hungry people who are hungry for *community...*" (emphasis mine)

As Asset Manager/Sponsors, we have chosen to partner with Apartment Life in our communities. This organization does an amazing job supporting the property manager by welcoming new tenants, connecting people together, and generally creating a happier place to call home. 93% of the apartment staffs surveyed nationally said that their programs increased the quality of life for their residents. *Check them out at www.ApartmentLife.org*

Regardless of your religion or background, if you agree that this is important and right, I urge you to partner with a Sponsor that sees life through a similar lens. And if you see it differently, that's ok, too.

Whatever you choose, I urge you to really get to know the Sponsor – the people – you write a check to and who you are trusting to write you many checks in return. There is no substitute for partnering with the right people. People who are trustworthy and knowledgeable. People who keep their word or nearly die trying. People who reap well because they've sown well. People who treat you, and their employees, contractors and tenants the way they wish to be treated. People who treat your dollars as well – or better – than their own.

There is no substitute for this type of relationship.

The Case for Investing in Multifamily Housing
By Sean Burton

The allure of trophy assets and high-profile office complexes can be difficult for an institutional investor to resist when allocating capital to real estate. Often overlooked are less flashy multifamily housing developments, which can be a more consistent source of long-term returns.

An institution's decision to favor office buildings is largely because of the profile of its tenant base. Office buildings can attract large, well-known companies that sign expensive, multiyear leases, whereas apartment buildings rely on numerous shorter-term tenants who may only commit to occupy the space for months at a time.

On paper, this longer duration bestows a sense of stability and creditworthiness to office buildings that multifamily projects appear to lack. But a closer look at the numbers reveals a different reality. Research from the National council of Real Estate Investment Fiduciaries shows that un-leveraged average returns from multifamily housing units have outpaced those of office buildings in four of the past five years — at times by more than 600 basis points. Why is this?

The most important reason multifamily developments frequently outperform their office counterparts is quite simple: consistent demand. Regardless of macro-economic conditions, people always need a place to live.

In a thriving economy, people can afford to live on their own and quickly fill housing that meets individual needs and brings them closer to jobs. During a down economy, renting may grow more attractive than buying for a variety of reasons: People lack the ability to save for a downpayment on a house, which may free them from ongoing home maintenance costs, and the short-term nature of renting provides location flexibility. These factors produce a reliable and stable revenue stream.

The same cannot be said of office developments. When times are good, office rent is consistent. However, during times of economic distress, businesses close, and those long-term leases, which looked so attractive on paper, can be broken or restructured. Empty offices are more difficult to lease as fewer businesses are launched or looking to move. The result: fewer tenants, less revenue.

Additionally, the fundamental nature of office space may be subject to disruptions with the advent of telecommuting and preferences for open floor plans or campus like environments. Offices built just 15 or 20 years ago can struggle to fit the needs of today's companies, which want more more creative and flexible spaces, rather than just private offices, conference rooms and cubicles. However, the functional, physical characteristics of homes have not changed: walls, roofs, living areas, bathrooms and kitchens.

A new office complex can have a dramatic impact on the local market. Just as a big buyer or seller of a thinly traded stock moves a company's share price up or down, the addition of hundreds of thousands — sometimes millions — of square feet of new office space can upset pricing as the market struggles to absorb new capacity. Conversely, the introduction of even the largest multifamily developments creates minimal disruption.

Ironically, it is precisely the makeup of the multifamily tenant base — lower-price short-term leases which institutional investors perceive as a negative — that may be its greatest strength. Unlike office buildings, multifamily developments are nimble enough to employ dynamic pricing models, much as airlines do when selling tickets for seats. Leasing prices in multifamily developments can be adjusted on a daily basis, up or down, depending on current demand and the available supply of units.

Office buildings are loath to adjust prices downward, especially when they are part of a publicly traded vehicle like a real estate investment trust, which can affect a stock price and produce inordinate consequences on commercial leases throughout the local market. The long duration of office leases can also hurt returns when buildings find themselves locked into agreements that were consummated at the bottom of the cycle, thereby depriving them of the ability to capture a market up-swing.

Last, the costs of putting a new, large tenant into an office space far exceed those of a new apartment renter because tenant improvements for offices are customized to the company and its aesthetic. Apartment renters may only expect fresh paint. As a result, multi-family developments can keep vacancy rates to a minimum, again ensuring a steady revenue stream.

Multifamily developments have another advantage for investors exiting a property. When office buildings are completed during down markets, investors suffer for two reasons: First, the value of for-sale assets will be considerably lower than original projections, which may have been calculated during more optimistic times. Second, properties built to be leased and held struggle to attract tenants, and lease terms will be set below originally anticipated prices.

By contrast, constant demand for multifamily housing and its use of dynamic pricing models mean that builders can ride out a downturn by continuing to rent the units and generate revenue. Assuming that the project is not over-leveraged, developers can hold the property, keeping it leased and generating cash flow, and sell when market conditions improve. This generates a more favorable sale price and increased returns.

Institutional investors by nature are long-term stewards of capital interested in generating consistent returns that meet the needs of their current and future obligations. To use a baseball analogy, institutions want a steady stream of singles and doubles and do not view themselves as home-run hitters, who also tend to strike out a lot. This long-term mandate to preserve and enhance capital philosophically matches up with the core characteristics of the multifamily asset class, which similarly seeks consistent performance with less volatility. Multifamily delivers that because of constant demand and the flexibility to quickly adjust pricing. This is a critical, yet often overlooked, consideration for institutional investors.

Ultimately, although multifamily developments may lack the superficial appeal of office buildings, the asset class warrants serious consideration for institutional investors deciding where to allocate capital within real estate.

Sean Burton is the president of CityView, a Los Angeles-headquartered developer and investment management firm focused on urban residential real estate in the western U.S.
Reprinted in Full with Permission of the Author

www.institutionalinvestor.com/blogarticle/3456887/blog/the-case-for-investing-in-multifamily-housing.html?ArticleID=3456887#/.V4_Djp-OgOko

Chapter 12 – Your Path to Investment Success

As I mentioned a number of times in these pages, I was awakened to the realm of commercial multifamily investing largely by the mistakes I made in past investments.

> ➤ I swung for the fences. Though I often hit it out of the park, like Babe Ruth, I struck out a number of times as well.

> ➤ I ignored the flies buzzing around a deal or investment sponsor. I found out later that something smelly down beneath kept them circling.

> ➤ I rushed too quickly into an opportunity without weighing all of the risks and alternatives.

Thankfully, I've enjoyed great success in many investments, particularly those in the multifamily and other commercial real estate realms. And thankfully, you don't have to repeat the mistakes I've made. Or the mistakes you've made in the past.

In this chapter, I want to walk through a step-by-step investment process that can assist you in making any investment decision. My friend, Chad Doty, laid out this process for me. Chad is the founder & CEO of the Multifamily Partner Program, based here in Virginia. You can look them up at www.multifamilypartner.com.

One of the worst ways to invest is to see what someone else has invested in, check it out, and sign up. You should first evaluate your situation to see if there is truly a fit between you and the investment, and see if the timing is right. Going through this process should help.

Don't try to start partway through this 7-step process.

Many people start at Step 5, then wonder why they don't get the results they hoped for. In fact, a lot of folks just do Step 6. Don't do that. Start at Step 1 for optimal results.

Step 1: Understand Your Current Assets. What do you have available? Is your investable capital working hard for you? Do you tolerate *lazy assets*? Are you getting 1 or 2% in a CD or bank account? If so, you are paying the bank a few percent for the privilege of holding your funds, because you're losing money to inflation.

What about *brokerage accounts*? Do you have pensions, IRAs, or 401(k)'s that are under-performing? What about trusts that have investable funds or assets that could be allocated differently? I have a Charitable Remainder Trust that was set up when we sold our company in 1997. Most of this trust is liquid, and I use the funds to invest in real estate. This can provide a better return than the mutual funds many trusts invest in.

Do you have *home equity* that could be safely utilized to increase your return? This used to sound irresponsible to me, because my parents' goal was to pay off their mortgage. But I found that I typically make many, many times the interest rate I'm charged and come out way ahead in the short and long run.

I purchased a home last month, and I had the option of getting a 90% mortgage. Instead, I jumped through a number of hoops to get a 60% first mortgage with a 30% second. The second mortgage is an equity line, and I can pay it down as low as I wish, or let it max out. This gives me the flexibility to keep it paid down most of the time, but to quickly tap into the cash if an investment opportunity arises. I'm currently paying under 5% interest on this line, and the investments I utilize it for usually make many times that.

What about *under-performing real estate*? There are cash-poor millionaires making zero to one or two percent on their investments. With good reallocation, they could safely be making 7 to 8% or more.

I had a piece of raw land that provided zero cash flow for years. I also had a lakefront vacation home that was fun, but provided a solid negative cash flow. After selling the home, I found that our family could take a fraction of the savings and rent great vacation homes in a variety of locations, and have funds left over to profitably invest. Don't get emotionally attached to real estate, and don't view it as a lottery ticket you hope will pay off. Because the odds of a big payday are often only a little better than gambling.

Other under-performing resources could include assets like precious metals. Though I used to view this asset class as insurance, rather than just an investment, I backed away from this thinking years ago. I have held precious metals for most of the last few decades, but after looking at the dismal returns last year, I sold my remaining positions. Look where precious metals fall on the risk & return graph in an earlier chapter. Dismal.

Step 2: Planning. After understanding your assets, you need to figure out what you want to achieve.

Are you looking for a *stable income stream* to live on or fund a life goal? Some investment advisors structure a program where principal is safely preserved and the yield is enjoyed by the investor throughout the rest of their life. This can be very effective. Real estate can provide this in a way that some other asset classes cannot.

Others are looking for *equity growth*. Some are growing their portfolio value for a major life event like retirement.

Some people are aiming for *wealth preservation and transfer*. Similar to equity growth, they may not require current income from the portfolio. Differently however, they are more concerned with protecting their downside than growing the upside.

In addition to the above, some are looking for a *tax shelter*. Many people have passive activity losses and need passive activity gains to consume them. Others have passive activity gains and need a shelter. Real estate can provide both depending on the investor's needs.

Step 3: Consider Your Investment Options. There are a variety of structures that could fit your needs and investment desires in the realm of commercial real estate.

You could consider a *REIT* (Real Estate Investment Trust). These can be publicly traded or privately held. REITs purchase real estate and have strict guidelines about how much of the income must be distributed to investors on a regular basis. If you require a lot of liquidity, this may be your best option. But this option comes with a number of downsides for most investors. If you can live without liquidity, you may be better working down the following list for higher profitability.

A *Limited Partnership* is a structure under which a general partner conducts business and utilizes limited partners to passively invest. Limited partners are liable for the business only to the extent of their cash investment (no debt), and they expect to receive periodic payments from cash flow. The general partner runs operations and his compensation is generally tied to the performance of the venture.

A *Master Limited Partnership* is similar to a limited partnership, but this investment is publicly traded. At least 90% of the MLP's cash flow must be derived from real estate, commodities or natural resources.

You can participate in an LLC as a *Direct Passive Fractional Owner* of the asset. This is the structure I have referred to, for the most part, in this volume. It is quite similar to the limited partnership I described above. This structure requires a trustworthy asset manager who will oversee the financial and operational aspects of your investment.

Correspondingly, you may choose to be a *Direct Owner*

and Asset Manager for these investments. This type of investor hires a staff or contracts with others (like a property management firm) to oversee the operations of the asset.

Lastly, some choose to be an *Owner **and** Active Manager.* This avenue provides the most control... has the highest potential profit...and may consume the lives of those who choose it. That might not be a bad thing if this is what you want to do as a full-time occupation.

As deal sponsors, my partner and I find ourselves in the role of Direct Owner and Asset Manager. The investors in our projects correspondingly function as Direct Passive Fractional Owners of an LLC or as Limited Partners in a Limited Partnership that we manage.

Step 4: Choose Your Partner. This is arguably the most important step of all. I've talked about this quite extensively already, but its importance makes it worth summarizing again here. (I am of course assuming that you plan to passively invest and the "partner" I'm referring to is the deal Sponsor and asset manager you will be entrusting to manage your investment and earn a profit.)

How did you hear about them? What is their *strategy and philosophy*? What are they trying to accomplish? Are they trying to create transactions and equity events? Build to sell? Generate long-term income? What do they want to do... and what does their company have a track record accomplishing?

Who are their principals? You must address this elephant in the room head-on. You need to be sure you're not investing with a crook. What have they done? How transparent is their reporting? What is their track record? There were dozens of clues about Bernie Madoff's indiscretions, but thousands of investors continually overlooked them.

You want to have *clarity about the performance history*. Madoff's records were apparently unclear about the flow of cash, views into the accounts, and more. You want to get clear reporting directly from the asset, where the title is on record, the third-party property manager is a fiduciary, with independent financial accounting, and the ability for them to show you both underlying reporting and their overall reporting at every step of the way. Getting this degree of clarity will help assure you that your money isn't going to end up in an undisclosed offshore account.

You need to understand their *growth forecasts* and their *experience*. You really need to understand who they are. Check them out carefully on social media. Ask for references. Check their SEC compliance. Some investors do criminal and civil background checks on their deal Sponsors. As deal Sponsors, we welcome this type of investigation. Anyone in this role should.

Step 5: What is Their Deal Review Process? Once you've screened your potential partner, check into the process they use to evaluate deals. Again, we've discussed this before, but it is critical.

What is their market and asset grade match? Are they a C grade owner in an emerging market? Great. Are they a developer in a slow or declining market? This might not make as much sense.

Sometimes a company's mission is to be a commercial real estate owner/manager in a certain geographic area. They may choose this so they learn their market and won't have to travel. Which makes sense. But it may also mean they become a jack-of-all-trades when it comes to asset class and approach. Which may not be optimal. This can create a sub-optimal return. Many of the best companies are laser-focused on an approach and an asset class and they park themselves in the markets that are providing the best context to succeed with that approach.

How do their financials stack up? What ripcords do they have? How can you exit a deal if you want to? Will they buy you out or provide other potential buyers? Have they ever had a cash call and how would this work? What can happen to your equity?

These issues aren't that hard to understand, but they can provide you important information about your returns and the safety of your investment.

Step 6: The Funding & Subscription Process. Once you've vetted a partner, and a deal, you may choose to invest. What process will you go through from this decision to the point of investing? Will you get full disclosure and 100% visibility into what you're investing in?

If this is a syndication, for example, a Private Placement Memorandum (PPM) and a Subscription Agreement should anchor your investment package. The PPM is basically a prospectus that reviews all of the potential risks and financials and legal obligations of both parties. You must sign off on the Subscription Agreement stating that you fully understand all of this.

Then you should understand where and how you're sending your funds. Are you sending funds to them? Or a clearing bank? And if so, how secure is the bank? And how long will your funds be parked until they actually go to the closing table?

What type of communications do they provide directly before and after closing? At year-end, do you get an annual report that is only an overview from them? Do you get quarterly or monthly reporting that includes the direct performance reporting straight from the asset? (We believe this should be the standard.)

Is there a clear startup process to onboard you as a new investor? All of these items tell you how much rigor this company has in their process and how well this company will likely take care of you and your money.

Step 7: Monitor and Track Your Investment. This is where the rubber meets the road. You've done all the hard work to evaluate your situation, your needs, the ideal investment structure, a deal partner and the deal. You've entrusted your hard-earned capital to them, and the excitement begins. Now it's time to hurry up and wait. Time to monitor and track the performance of your investment.

I quoted this earlier in the book, but I love the saying so much that I'm repeating it here.

"Investing should be more like watching paint dry or watching grass grow. If you want excitement, take $800 and go to Las Vegas."

Paul Samuelson – *First American Winner of Nobel Prize in Economic Sciences*

How accurate and complete is their reporting? Are their distributions performed on their published cycle? Do you have options on how you receive your distribution... mail, wire or ACH bank transfer? How do they do tax reporting?

How do they do performance reporting? Once you invest, do you ever speak with them again? Do you hear from them once or twice annually? Do your expectations for communications match their style? Do their investors ever feel like they're in the dark?

Summary

As I mentioned earlier, you should go through all of these steps prior to investing. Never start at step 5 or 6 then wonder why step 7 is not going well.

A broker can sell you anything and they will make a commission. It may be a great investment. But is it a great investment *for you*? Only you can ultimately answer that. I hope this process assists you in that endeavor.

Chapter 13 – Closing Thoughts...The Perfect Investment?

On the cover of this volume and in Chapter 1, I made a claim that you may have considered arrogant: *I'm writing this book to tell you about The Perfect Investment.*

Have I convinced you?

I urged you to stop swinging for the fences. We talked about how the super-wealthy acquired and maintain their wealth – so often through commercial real estate, which is hard to access by the majority of investors.

We discussed the historic convergence of demographic trends and government regulatory faux pas that have fueled the profitability and stability of this sector. We have favorably compared the multifamily asset class to stocks, REITs, precious metals and the other commercial asset classes. We saw how multifamily fared positively to single family housing and other asset classes in the recent recession, and how the nature of multifamily housing generally provides a buffer during any downturn.

I demonstrated the four pillars of return and growth in the multifamily arena (Cash Flow, Appreciation, Principal Pay-down, and Tax Advantages), and we took a deep dive into the surprisingly rich tax benefits experienced by most multifamily investors. We talked about the importance of finding a high integrity deal partner, and the steps every investor should take when evaluating a new investment.

So were you convinced?

Think about this... there's at least one more reason that *The Perfect Investment* is so perfect. **It's a win-win for every party involved**.

So many purchases, investments, relationships, and other transactions in our lives involve a disproportionate benefit to one party over another. Sometimes it's clear upfront... other times it's not.

Not so with commercial multifamily. Done right, **everybody wins.**

> ➤ **The Seller wins.** It's a growing market, and with very few exceptions, sellers are realizing sizable gains when taking their asset to market. As Sponsors, we don't have to "steal" a property to get a good deal.

> ➤ **The Broker wins.** Commercial multifamily brokers work hard and they are well-compensated for their work in putting buyers and sellers together and bringing transactions to consummation.

> ➤ **The Investors win.** As we've discussed at length, investors in commercial multifamily are experiencing some of the strongest returns with the lowest risk and highest stability available on the planet.

> ➤ **The Sponsor wins.** I'm proud to be a Sponsor of commercial multifamily projects, and thrilled to play a role in bringing joy and prosperity to the other parties on this list. I'm also delighted to see my family prosper and to positively impact culture by providing significant funding to the organizations and people on my *BIG WHY* list.

> ➤ **Our Tenants win.** My team has a sincere desire to make apartment units into homes, and to connect homes together to build communities. To make life better for our tenants. Tenants of well-run multifamily properties win.

> ➤ **Our Vendors and their Employees win.** A well-run multifamily business creates rewarding opportunities

for property management teams, financial and legal staff, bankers and more.

Everybody wins. You could call it a Win-Win-Win-Win-Win-Win.

So what about you? Are you ready to learn more about *The Perfect Investment?* I would love to chat with you. Please visit us online at wellingscapital.com, and contact me directly at paul@wellingscapital.com or at 1-800-844-2188.

Appendix A – Introduction to Wellings Capital

A practical way to create enduring wealth through the historic shift to commercial multifamily housing. We can help you achieve your long-term financial goals by providing access to invest in commercial multifamily apartment projects in growing US markets.

As real estate investors and investment sponsors, we have long been aware of the need for a profitable investment that is safe, predictable and based on a hard asset.

Wellings Capital meets this need in at least 6 ways…

1. Principal Preservation. The security of your original investment is our primary focus. This is investing rule #1: "First, lose no money."

2. Stable Cash Returns. Our investments are structured to generate steady, quarterly income.

3. Increasing Cash Returns. It is our goal to increase the operating performance of the property every month. This is reflected in Net Operating Income (NOI) growth. When we improve operations, we improve net cash back to our investors.

4. Growing Equity. By growing rent, improving the property and paying down principal, your equity can increase steadily over time.

5. Opportunity to Accelerate. Our investors benefit from equity harvesting over time to create accelerated jumps in yield. Through the use of strategic refinancing and tax-deferred exchanges upon sale, our investors increase income at higher than normal rates. This is possible because equity invariably grows faster than income. Excess equity can be harvested and redeployed into more projects without additional cash from our investors. The result: multiple assets increasing in value and providing yield from one initial investment.

6. Multiple Tax Advantages. As owners of real multifamily assets, our investors get access to a variety of IRS-sanctioned tax-reducing and avoidance opportunities.

We invest in high performing, value-add properties that provide you with cash flow and equity growth throughout the life of the investment. The portfolio consists of B- to B+ assets in stable and growing markets across the United States.

We are an income-focused real estate investment firm whose goal is to provide stable, yield-producing investments to our clients. Our founders have over 100 years of combined business and management experience and a lifelong history of client satisfaction and performance.

We follow a reliable blueprint: an active, personalized approach to portfolio management coupled with a conservative investment philosophy. Translation: **Wellings Capital gives you access to a Multi-Generational Wealth Engine**.

One More Critical Investment Rule…

For every investment, we also consider the "Golden Rule."

It may not sound overly sophisticated, but this enduring principle started with the world's greatest Teacher, and has been proven over and over again in companies and relationships and hard decisions all over the world for 2,000 years.

For every project, before we sign the Purchase Agreement, we pause and ask ourselves and each other...

"Would we put our own family's last $100,000 in this project?"

Please note, we don't advocate putting any amount of "last dollars" into anything but a liquid savings account, BUT it is a very useful construct.

It keeps our investment decisions centered on what's most important: **You.**

To learn more about our investment philosophy, you can contact us at **1-800-844-2188** or visit us at **www.wellingscap-ital.com.**

You can also email me at paul@wellingscapital.com.

Appendix B

An Interview with Tech Investor/Entrepreneur Wade T. Myers

This is the candid narrative of how respected investor and entrepreneur, Wade T. Myers, went from real estate skeptic... to writing the endorsement on my back cover... to actually throwing himself into the multifamily arena. This section ends with a brief interview Mr. Myers as well.

Before proceeding, let me give you a brief overview of Mr. Myers's background. Wade grew up with a Mennonite background in the badlands of western North Dakota with no electricity or indoor plumbing. After working his way through college, Wade was an active duty officer in the U.S. Army where he was an Army Ranger and commanded a special weapons assault platoon. During his time in the Army Wade received a master's degree in computer information services from Texas A&M. After his service, he quickly climbed the ranks at Mobil Chemical, eventually leading a large product division.

Wade was recalled to active duty to serve in the 1991 Gulf War, where he was an Arab liaison to the Northern Arab Command and was the engineer operations executive that coordinated Saudi support for 600,000 U.S. troops. He received the Bronze Star for his service and returned home to enter Harvard Business School where he graduated as a Baker Scholar (top 5% of his MBA class).

While working as a top strategy consultant at the Boston Consulting Group (BCG) after grad school, his work included leading the foundational strategy for the largest Internet-based travel agency and for the first ticketless airline process for the largest US-based airline, both of which helped transform the travel industry. Inspired by what could be done with a combination of strategy and technology, Wade left BCG to become a tech entrepreneur. As a venture-backed entrepreneur, Wade has founded, co-founded, or invested in over 35 startups, including a global internet services firm capitalized with $75 million whose all-star investor list included Michael Dell. Another firm he founded and currently chairs is a tech-enabled real estate services firm that is an Inc. 5000 firm and in the top 10 out of 6,500 firms in its industry. Wade has led 55 financings and/or mergers and acquisitions as part of his business building activities.

Wade has become a popular speaker in the U.S., Europe, Asia, and the Middle East on topics related to entrepreneurship and investments. You can read more about him at Wade-TMyers.com.

I met Wade at a conference in 2008, and we stayed in touch over the years. In 2011 and 2012, I unsuccessfully pitched Wade on investing in a multifamily development and a Hyatt House hotel that we built in the Midwest. "I'm really focused on tech," he said. "I don't have a deep level of knowledge about commercial real estate."

It wasn't until several years later that Wade confessed that he had been burned in his early 20's through a few small real estate investments.

When I finished the draft of this book, I approached Wade for an endorsement. His exact response to my text was, "Sure. If that is useful to you."

Now I was born at night... but it wasn't last night. I could read between the lines of his response. Translation: "I really don't want to, but I value our friendship, so I'll take a quick look at it."

I sent the draft over to Wade, hoping to get some response within a week or two. Two or three hours later, I was surprised to get his enthusiastic email. He had read the first five chapters, and skimmed the rest. Not only did he write an enthusiastic endorsement (see back cover), but he also asked about investing with our company.

"Wait a minute," I thought. "Wasn't this Wade Myers? One of the most prominent entrepreneurs I know? The man who hadn't seriously looked at the last two or three deals I sent his way?"

Over the next several months, Wade and I continued conversations. Though I could never have anticipated it when I first approached him, Wade eventually joined our firm as a partner.

Just like the guy on TV who said, "I liked the product so much, I bought the company." The stability and demographics of the multifamily sector were powerful enough to not only erase 30+ years of skepticism about commercial real estate investing, but also convinced Wade to actually broaden his entrepreneurial and investment focus to join our company as a partner!

It may seem odd that I would use a business partner's blurb on my own book cover. Self-serving in a way (you would certainly never accuse me of that, now would you?). But hopefully this little narrative gives a little background.

My business partner, Brian Robbins, and I are thrilled to have Wade join us. If you would like to learn more, and consider joining us as a passive multifamily investor, please contact me today at paul@WellingsCapital.com.

Here's my short interview with Wade...

Interview with Wade T. Myers

Q: You are a tech entrepreneur and investor, is that correct?

Y: Yes. While I was working at the Boston Consulting Group, I discovered the powerful combination of strategy, business process redesign, technology, capital, creativity, and leadership and how that combination can be transformative. That's basically all that I've done as an entrepreneur and as an investor since then.

Q: What kind of outcomes have you experienced?

Y: The typical bell curve that you would expect from early-stage tech companies: a few smash hits that returned 10x to 20x, one bust that only returned part of the capital, some that were minimal returns and most were adequate returns.

Q: So you've had some big successes that are really impressive...

Y: Yes and over time, with more experience, I've seen the top of the bell curve skew to the right with better outcomes, but there are still many variables such as market, product, competition, etc. that lead to a broad distribution of outcomes, so there is never any guarantee of an outcome.

Q: And now you are shifting more of your energy and resources into multifamily property investing, right?

A: That is correct. I've been very focused in the past, but I am branching out now into the multifamily sector.

Q: Can you explain why you've added multifamily investing as you branched out instead of other investment options?

A: Well first of all, everyone should pursue a broad asset allocation strategy when investing their money, but when it comes to being an entrepreneur, focus is critical so that you can fully leverage lessons learned from previous experience into the next venture. One of the tools I developed to help me focus my tech efforts was an opportunity analysis that included 50 key principles that helped determine success vs. failure. When that analysis is applied to the multifamily sector, the sector scores astonishingly high compared to other entrepreneurial pursuits. Importantly, the bell curve has much shorter tails and a much higher normal distribution with most outcomes being really good returns. So while there are no 10x+ returns (call them Grand Slams), it is much more certain that you will hit lots of doubles and triples with far fewer strikeouts.

Q: What is different about the multifamily sector that makes it such a good investment?

A: Multifamily has always been an attractive sector with decent returns, but in the last few years, the dynamics of the housing industry writ large, including the rise of the cost of housing, the difficulty of getting a mortgage, the rising demand for housing, and the tax advantages of real estate investing, have all shifted to make the sector much more attractive as a target investment than ever before. And in terms of the risks of any competitive advantages getting "competed away" by a newer, better technology that renders your tech investment worthless – which happens all the time in the tech sector – the real estate based nature of multifamily means it is nearly impossible to be surprised by a competitive move that suddenly renders your investment useless.

Appendix C

My *BIG WHY*

I mentioned that everyone should have a BIG WHY to keep them moving forward in any entrepreneurial or investment enterprise. That one burning desire that keeps you focused when potential distractions rage on every side, or when setbacks tempt you to quit. I promised to tell you about mine.

This Appendix isn't really about multifamily investing. But it is for me. And I'm guessing it will resonate with many of you as well.

The BIG WHY... For some it's wealth. For others it's free time and leisure. Some want to leave a legacy or an inheritance for their children's children. These are great, and commercial multifamily can accomplish all of these things and more.

I'd like to do all these, but I've got something that drives me much more.

I believe we were created in the image of a brilliant Designer. He has the perfect answers to all of the world's problems.

And anyone who looks around can see there are a lot of problems. It didn't start out that way, and it's His stated plan that it won't end that way either.

Since He has the answers to all of these problems, and He made us in His image (He was looking in a mirror when He created you!), it logically follows that we are His Plan A to fix this broken planet. I believe He wants to partner with us to solve the world's problems.

So put very simply, that is the thinking behind my BIG WHY. My life ambition is to harness resources to fix the broken systems of this world.

➤ To put orphans in homes.

➤ To turn the tide of human trafficking and slavery.

➤ To feed the hungry and raise the standard of living for the impoverished around the world.

➤ To increase literacy in 3rd world nations.

➤ And to tell every single human being that I contact that they are valuable. They are unique. That they are loved. That they are a priceless treasure.

As we own and operate apartments, we are already serving humanity in a number of important ways…

➤ We provide a safe and happy place for thousands of individuals and families to live.

➤ We provide safe and profitable investments for hundreds of investors.

➤ We provide secure and well-paying jobs for our staff and property management teams.

➤ We provide current income and profitable investments for our families.

That would be enough to call it a day and feel satisfied in a job well done. That would be enough "whys" to keep me moving forward.

But I have traveled to third world nations. I have held Haitian children whose parents were crushed under a cruel earthquake's rubble. I've smelled the polluted air of Katmandu and I've held the hands of Nicaraguan beggars who have nothing. I have mourned over the impoverished and sick and lonely from rural China to inner city Detroit.

I can't rest while children are being enslaved and terrorists ravage families and people groups for fun.

If you get to know me, you'll soon find out where I invest my resources... my time, my energy and my income. I've spent a lot of pages telling you about my journey in multifamily investing. I thought I should take a few pages to share about why I do what I do. Thank you for taking the time to read this, and I hope and pray the very best for you in everything you do.

About the Author

After graduating with an engineering degree and then an MBA from Ohio State, Paul entered the management development track at Ford Motor Company in Detroit. He later departed to start a staffing company with a partner. Before selling it to a publicly traded firm five years later, Paul was Finalist for Ernst & Young's Michigan Entrepreneur of the Year 2 years straight.

Paul later entered the real estate sector, where he flipped over 40 homes and 25 high-end waterfront lots, rehabbed and managed rental properties, built a number of new homes, developed a subdivision, and created two successful online real estate marketing firms. He also built a number of other companies and made quite a few medium- and high-risk investments along the way. Some paid off while others did not. Lessons learned during the downturn led him to the relative stability of the commercial real estate sector. Three successful developments, including assisting with development of a Hyatt hotel, a high-end office building, and the development, financing, and asset management of a successful commercial multifamily housing project led him into this arena.

After a careful analysis of historical commercial risks and returns, Paul and his partner, Dr. Brian Robbins, narrowed their focus to stabilized Class B apartments in growing markets. Their multi-generational wealth engine has opened the door for passive investors to enjoy the unique safety, tax advantages, and profitability of the commercial multifamily investment class.

More recently, Paul joined a team of entrepreneurs, educators, and pastors to form 7MountainSchool.com. This school holds an optimistic view of the future for America and the world, and mentors young people to move boldly into various spheres of society to bring positive, lasting change.

A large portion of the profit from Paul's business is funneled into 7 Mountain and other world-changing initiatives. These include putting orphans in homes, ending human trafficking, and raising the standard of living for the impoverished around the world.